ALL-AMERICAN TRIVIA

Moments
TO
Remember
IN
History

Independence
Days

Publications International, Ltd.

Compiled and written by **Margaret McConnell.**

Additional research and writing by **Debra Almgren-Horwitz, Alyssa Amedei,** and **Sarah Gorr.**

Image credits: Art Explosion, JupiterImages, Library of Congress, PIL collection, Shutterstock, Thinkstock

Cover images: Thinkstock

ISBN-13: 978-1-4508-4650-9
ISBN-10: 1-4508-4650-5

Manufactured in USA.

8 7 6 5 4 3 2 1

CONTENTS

★ ★ ★ ★ ★ ★ ★ ★ ★ ★ ★ ★ ★ ★ ★ ★

DISCOVERY

★ ★ ★ ★ ★ ★ ★ ★ ★ ★ ★ ★

**From land and space discoveries to technological inventions,
the progress of any nation depends on
exploration and discovery.**

Q. When did humans first set foot on the land that would become the United States?

A. Researchers (archaeologists, geneticists, and linguists) believe humans first wandered into Alaska by crossing a land bridge from Asia approximately 13,000 years ago. Humans likely crossed over the land bridge as they hunted for mammals.

TRUE OR FALSE Almost 500 years before Columbus sailed the ocean blue, Vikings not only landed, but also settled in North America.

ANSWER True. Around A.D. 1005 Thorfinn and Gudrid Karlsefni led a group of homesteaders that numbered between 65 and 265. They came with livestock and supplies to settle what they called "Vineland," and they stayed for two years. Conflicts with the native people caused them to leave.

Q. Did Columbus ever set foot on the land that would one day be the United States of America?

A. Columbus never disembarked on United States soil. During his famous 1492 trip, Columbus reached only the islands of the Caribbean (and returned home to tell everyone he'd found the outer islands of China!). Historians still hold Columbus in high esteem, though, because his voyages proved to the Europeans that such exploration was feasible. Columbus's voyages directly led to the first European settlements in North America.

⭐ Some historians believe Columbus became familiar with stories about the Viking voyages to the New World when he ended up in Iceland after being attacked by pirates during his 1477 voyage. Just as many historians doubt Columbus was ever in Iceland, however.

TRUE OR FALSE Spanish explorers brought the first horses to North America.

ANSWER False. Modern horses lived in the Americas up to 3 million years ago. They disappeared approximately 10,000 years ago for reasons unknown (speculations run the gamut from disease to hunting). Spanish explorers *reintroduced* horses to the Americas in 1519.

Q. When was the oldest continuously inhabited city in North America settled?

A. Spanish explorer Pedro Menéndez de Avilés stepped off his ship in Spanish Florida on August 28, 1565—the feast day of St. Augustine of Hippo. Menendez named the settlement he founded St. Augustine in the saint's honor.

Q. In what year did colonist John White establish the legendary Roanoke colony?

A. John White established the Roanoke colony in July 1587. It consisted of 88 men, 17 women, and 11 children. The colony found itself low on

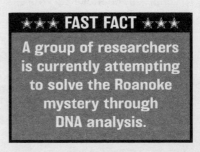

★★★ **FAST FACT** ★★★

A group of researchers is currently attempting to solve the Roanoke mystery through DNA analysis.

supplies within months, and it was decided that White would return to England to gather more supplies. White's return mission to Roanoke was complicated by warfare between England and Spain. When he finally returned to Roanoke in 1590, the colony had been deserted.

What Became of the Lost Colony?

★ ★ ★ ★ ★ ★ ★ ★ ★ ★ ★ ★

No one knows what happened to the Roanoke colonists, but speculation abounds. It's possible the colonists traveled to another island or to the mainland. It's even possible that the colonists tried to sail back to England. If so, they likely perished at sea. Yet there are at least a few shreds of hearsay evidence that the colonists survived in America.

John Smith

In 1607, Captain John Smith established the first successful English settlement in North America at Jamestown, Virginia. The colony's secretary, William Strachey, wrote four years later about hearing a report of four English men, two boys, and one young woman who had been sighted south of Jamestown at a settlement of the Eno tribe, where they were being used as slaves. If the report was true, who else could these English have been but Roanoke survivors?

In the intervening centuries, many of the individual tribes of the region have disappeared. Some died out, others were absorbed into larger groups. One surviving group, the Lumbee, often have Caucasian features. Could they be descendants of Roanoke colonists? Many among the Lumbee dismiss the notion, but the tribe has long been thought to be of mixed heritage and has been speaking English so long that none among them know what language preceded it.

Q. When was Harvard University (the oldest institution of higher learning in the United States) founded?

A. Harvard was founded as New College by the Massachusetts Bay Colony in 1636. It was renamed Harvard College in 1638 after John Harvard bequeathed his estate to the institution.

Q. What 1793 invention dramatically transformed the American South?

A. Eli Whitney's cotton gin removed the seeds from cotton and made mass production of the South's cotton possible—and thus cotton production more profitable. Southern cotton plantations were soon shipping massive amounts of cotton to New England and Europe.

★★★ **FAST FACT** ★★★

Eli Whitney said he came up with the idea for the cotton gin as he observed a cat trying to pull a chicken through a fence. Whitney took note of the fact that the cat was successful only at pulling a few feathers through the fence.

Q. When did the first documented gold find in the United States take place?

A. Gold was found at Reed Farm in Midland, North Carolina, in 1799.

Q. When did the United States purchase Louisiana from France?

A. In April 1803, the United States, under President Thomas Jefferson, purchased the 828,000 square miles of land from France.

Q. When did Lewis and Clark embark upon their amazing journey?

A. Lewis and Clark set out on the Missouri River from St. Louis on May 21, 1804. President Thomas Jefferson sent them to explore the lands of the Louisiana Purchase and to search for a direct water route to the Pacific Ocean (the fabled Northwest Passage). Lewis and Clark made an efficient team, with Clark in charge of charting and mapping the course and Lewis focused on studying and logging the flora and fauna of the new areas.

⭐ On April 29, 1805, Lewis and another member of the expedition party killed a grizzly bear in Montana. Before Lewis had seen one of the bears with his own eyes, he had thought the Native Americans had exaggerated their tales about the beasts. After his own encounters with the bears, he clearly understood what his guides had been trying to tell him.

Q. When did the Lewis and Clark expedition arrive back in St. Louis?

A. Lewis and Clark returned to St. Louis on September 23, 1806. The townspeople were amazed to see them—they had basically been given up for dead after being gone for two and a half years.

Q. Who is credited with developing the first commercially practical steamboat in 1807?

A. On August 17, 1807, Robert Fulton's steamboat *Clermont* left New York City and arrived in Albany 32 hours later. With this maiden voyage, Fulton proved that this mode of transportation could be faster than land travel.

Q. What event in 1825 put New York on the path to becoming the "Empire State"?

A. The opening of the Erie Canal was surely the monumental event of the year for New York. The idea of a canal to connect the Eastern Seaboard with the lands farther west had been batted around for years when entrepreneur Jesse Hawley presented a plan to President Thomas Jefferson. Jefferson rejected the expensive plan as "a little short of madness," but New York Governor DeWitt Clinton was more receptive. The plan was quickly labeled "Clinton's Folly," but Governor Clinton surely got the last laugh. The new canal put New York on the path to becoming a center of international trade.

Q. What useful device was invented on a Virginia farm in 1831?

A. The mechanical reaper. Cyrus McCormick invented this reaper by improving upon his father's design. Sales of the machine were slow at first but picked up after Cyrus moved operations to Chicago in 1847. Midwestern farmers came out in droves to purchase the new tools.

Q. What find caused great excitement at Sutter's Mill in Coloma, California, in 1848?

A. Pioneer John Sutter and his partner James W. Marshall found flakes of gold on January 24, 1848, setting off the California gold rush.

Q. When was the Comstock Lode discovered, and what was the significance of this new find?

A. The Comstock Lode was discovered in the spring of 1859. It was the first major silver discovery in the United States, and the silver that was mined helped fund the Union during the Civil War.

Q. When was the first transcontinental telegraph sent, and which American cities were involved?

A. On October 24, 1861, Chief Justice of California Cyrus Field sent the first transcontinental telegraph from San Francisco to President Abraham Lincoln in Washington, D.C. It read: "[This line] will be the means of strengthening the

Tragedy Leads to the Telegraph
★ ★ ★ ★ ★ ★ ★ ★ ★ ★ ★ ★

Samuel F. B. Morse, inventor of the electrical telegraph, was originally a painter. He became interested in telegraphy after a personal tragedy. While in Washington, D.C., at work on a portrait of the Marquis de Lafayette, Morse received a letter from his father in Connecticut via horse messenger that simply read, "Your dear wife is convalescent." Morse dropped everything and rushed to his wife,

Samuel F. B. Morse

Lucretia. By the time he reached her, she had passed away. A heartbroken Morse found solace in his search for a means of rapid long-distance communication.

attachment which binds both the East and the West to the Union." This event made the Pony Express obsolete.

Q. When was the golden spike driven to complete the iconic transcontinental railroad?

A. The golden spike was driven on May 10, 1869, at Promontory Summit, Utah. A telegraph announced the news, and the nation let out a collective cheer. Shipping items from coast to coast was suddenly simpler and cheaper, as was settlement of the West.

Q. When did Alexander Graham Bell make his famous phone call to his assistant Thomas Watson?

A. Bell called Watson on March 10, 1876, and said, "Mr. Watson, come here, I want to see you." Their conversation marked the first successful bi-directional transmission of clear speech.

★ In the spring of 1930, a group of senators tried to ban all dial telephones from the Senate wing of the Capitol, as the technophobic older senators found them too complicated to use.

Q. Can prolific inventor Thomas Edison take the credit for inventing the lightbulb?

A. Thomas Edison did not invent the lightbulb, but the lightbulb he created in 1879 lasted longer and was more efficient than any of the earlier lightbulbs.

Q. Which Chicago structure qualified as the first skyscraper?

A. Chicago's Home Insurance Building, designed by William Le Baron Jenney and built in 1884, was the world's first skyscraper. It stood ten stories tall and relied on an interior steel frame to bear the load of the building, which allowed the exterior walls to be lighter and the building to be taller. This innovation is still used in the designs of modern skyscrapers.

★ Elisha Otis's improvements on the design of elevators (most notable: safety mechanisms) allowed for the advent of the skyscraper era.

Q. What happened on January 10, 1901, near Beaumont, Texas?

A. Spindletop dome erupted on this date in 1901 to set off the Texas oil boom. The geyser of oil erupted more than 100 feet into the air, and it took nine days for workers to bring it under control.

★ At Spindletop, Anthony F. Lucas proved that rotary drilling could cut through deep, hardened layers of rock, and that these depths could contain large pockets of petroleum oil.

Q. What 1902 invention greatly improved quality of life throughout the world?

A. Willis Carrier invented the first air-conditioning system in 1902. The grateful recipient was Sackett-Wilhelms Lithographing & Publishing Company of Brooklyn, New York.

> ★★★ **FAST FACT** ★★★
>
> At the 1939 New York World's Fair, the Carrier Corporation building was a giant igloo.

⭐ The advent of air-conditioning drastically changed life in the United States. Prior to the invention, scores of citizens spent a great deal of time outdoors during hot weather. Air-conditioning gave people a choice on hot days.

TRUE OR FALSE The Model T was the first automobile.

ANSWER False. The Model T was not the first automobile, but it was noteworthy because it was the first automobile that a lot of people could afford. Before the Model T, only wealthy people had cars.

★★★ **FAST FACT** ★★★

The Model T was often affectionately referred to as "Tin Lizzie."

Q. When did the first person drive across the United States in an automobile?

A. 1903. Dr. Horatio Nelson Jackson completed the first transcontinental crossing of the United States by car. He was accompanied by his dog and a mechanic. The trip took 65 days, and all three wore goggles during the excursion.

⭐ The Lincoln Highway was the first road that ran across the United States. It opened in 1913 and ran from Times Square in New York City to Lincoln Park in San Francisco. The Lincoln Highway no longer exists, but I-80 roughly follows its old route.

Q. When was Honolulu connected to San Francisco via undersea telegraph cables?

A. On January 1, 1903, the Commercial Pacific Cable Company opened the first direct telegraph connection between Honolulu and San Francisco.

⭐ Before Honolulu was connected to San Francisco via undersea telegraph cables, all messages were sent from the East Coast through Capetown and the Indian Ocean.

Q. What happened in Kitty Hawk, North Carolina, on December 17, 1903?

A. Brothers Orville and Wilbur Wright made the first manned flight in an engine-powered airplane on this date. They flew 852 feet in 59 seconds, reaching an altitude of 15 feet.

> ★★★ **FAST FACT** ★★★
>
> The United States bought the land that would become New Mexico and Arizona from Mexico in the Gadsden Purchase of 1853.

Q. Which two Southwest states became part of the Union in 1912?

A. New Mexico and Arizona. They were the last to join the Union until 1959.

Q. Which United States president was the first to appear on television?

A. Franklin Delano Roosevelt achieved this presidential first when he appeared on television during the opening ceremonies of the New York World's Fair in 1939.

Q. When was the first computer used, and what types of computations was it used for?

A. The first general-purpose electric computer was called ENIAC (Electronic Numerical Integrator And Computer). The United States Army began using it in 1946 for various computations, such as calculating artillery firing tables.

Q. When did work commence on the Interstate Highway System?

A. President Dwight D. Eisenhower signed the Federal Aid Highway Act into law in June 1956. Roadwork began later that summer.

★ A common myth is that one of every five miles in the Interstate Highway System is straight so these straight areas can serve as runways in the event of a national emergency. This simply is not true, and historians are not sure how this rumor originated.

Q. What was notable about executive orders 10823 and 10860 of 1959?

A. These executive orders added stars to the flag in honor of Alaska and Hawaii, which both achieved statehood in 1959.

> ★★★ **FAST FACT** ★★★
> The United States originally purchased Alaska from Russia in 1867.

★ There is nothing in the Constitution that specifically permits executive orders, but the practice of issuing executive orders derives from a mention of "executive power" in the Constitution. Most presidents have used executive orders to clarify or further existing laws rather than to make any new laws.

Q. What noteworthy goal did President Kennedy announce in 1962?

A. Kennedy announced that his goal was for the United States to send a man to the moon by the end of the decade.

"Those who came before us made certain that this country rode the first waves of the industrial revolutions . . . and this generation does not intend to founder in the backwash of the coming age of space."
—President John F. Kennedy, September 12, 1962

Q. When was President Kennedy's goal realized, and who realized it?

A. On July 21, 1969, U.S. astronaut Neil Armstrong stepped off the *Apollo 11* landing craft and stepped onto the surface of the moon—making President Kennedy's goal a reality.

★ Since the 1940s, the United States and Russia have both tentatively explored the idea of using nuclear-powered rockets to achieve a manned mission to Mars.

Q. When was an automated teller machine (ATM) first used in the United States?

A. The first ATM in the United States started dispensing money at Chemical Bank on Long Island in New York in 1969.

> ★★★ **FAST FACT** ★★★
>
> Don Wetzel, a Dallas executive, came up with the idea for ATMs as he stood in line at a bank in 1968.

GOLDEN LEGENDS

★ ★ ★ ★ ★ ★ ★ ★ ★ ★ ★ ★

These are the giants—the events upon which this great nation was built. From the Boston Tea Party and the Declaration of Independence to Martin Luther King Jr.'s speech, these are the moments Americans call to mind with pride.

Q. What notable event was led by American patriot (and failed brewer) Samuel Adams?

A. The Boston Tea Party. The colonists were never fond of the taxes imposed by the British government. Parliament had passed a number of tax acts, but when the British levied a tax on tea imported into the colonies, the colonists decided they had had enough. One night in December 1773, Adams and a group of Boston patriots boarded three Royal vessels and tossed 342 crates of tea into Boston Harbor.

★ Because the patriots inadvertently chose to execute the Boston Tea Party at low tide, the crates of tea piled up in the shallow water after the colonists threw them overboard. The colonists had to jump into the water and actually smash open the crates to make sure the tea was ruined.

TRUE OR FALSE Paul Revere never reached his destination of Concord, Massachusetts, on his famed midnight ride.

ANSWER True. On April 18, 1775, Revere and two others left Boston on horseback to warn residents of Concord that the British were coming. British spies detained Revere and another rider, while the third rider successfully warned Concord.

Q. What anonymous document was published on January 9, 1776?

A. Thomas Paine's pamphlet *Common Sense*. Paine went on to sell 500,000 copies of the document, which greatly advanced the cause of American independence.

The Attack on the HMS *Gaspee*

★ ★ ★ ★ ★ ★ ★ ★ ★ ★ ★ ★

Eighteen months before the Boston Tea Party, the British revenue schooner HMS *Gaspee* was burned by American patriots near Providence, Rhode Island. The motive behind the attack was resentment and distrust of British efforts to regulate trade—it came on the heels of a series of taxes put into effect by the British in 1764.

The colonists viewed the *Gaspee*, which was moored in Narragansett Bay, as a symbol of British heavy-handedness. Sent to enforce customs collections and to inspect colonial vessels, the ship provoked immediate resentment. On June 9, 1772, the *Gaspee* grounded as it chased a ship; the colonists knew the *Gaspee* would be stuck where it was until high tide, and they took full advantage of the golden opportunity. Under the canopy of a moonless night, a group of angry patriots boarded the ship.

In the ensuing scuffle, the ship's commander was wounded by musket fire and forced to surrender his vessel. He was placed in a rowboat, and he and his crew went ashore. The patriots then burned the ship within full sight of cheering colonists gathered along the shoreline. No one was killed in the incident, which was a sign of the patriots' good faith. Theirs was simply a symbolic act against a system they believed was unfair.

Q. What momentous event that Americans commemorate every year took place on July 4, 1776?

A. The Continental Congress approved the Declaration of Independence on this date in 1776.

When, in the course of human events, it becomes necessary for one people to dissolve the political bands which have connected them with another, and to assume among the powers of the earth, the separate and equal station to which the laws of nature and of nature's God entitle them, a decent respect to the opinions of mankind requires that they should declare the causes which impel them to separation.

—Opening words of the Declaration of Independence

Q. On what date was patriot Nathan Hale hanged?

A. September 22, 1776. When General Washington requested a volunteer for a mission behind enemy lines, Hale eagerly stepped forward. Disguised as a teacher looking for work, Hale relayed information to the

Nathan Hale

Americans about British troop movement. He was captured on September 21 and was hanged by the British for espionage the following day.

★ It is believed that Hale's cousin Samuel Hale, who was a loyalist serving with British troops, detected his cousin in disguise and gave him up to the British.

Q. When was the bald eagle chosen as the national bird?

A. June 20, 1782. The bald eagle was chosen as a prominent symbol because of its long life, great strength, and majestic appearance.

⭐ Benjamin Franklin disliked the choice of the bald eagle as the national bird. Franklin said the eagle was "a bird of bad moral character. He does not get his living honestly.... He watches the labor of the fishing hawk; and when that diligent bird has at length taken a fish, and is bearing it to his nest for the support of his mate and young ones, the bald eagle pursues him, and takes it from him."

Q. When did the Constitution replace the Articles of Confederation?

A. March 4, 1789. The Articles of Confederation were the first constitution of the United States. They called for a weak central government, with most of the power in the hands of the states. The federal government had little real power—it could not collect taxes or regulate domestic or international trade, for instance. Difficulties quickly arose under the Articles of Confederation, with the federal government struggling to pay off debts incurred during the Revolutionary War and the states competing against each other to trade with other countries. The present Constitution addressed the weaknesses inherent in the Articles of Confederation—and replaced them on March 4, 1789.

Q. When were the *Federalist Papers* published?

A. The *Federalist Papers* were published from 1787 to 1788. They were written for New York newspapers under the pen name "Publius" by Alexander Hamilton, John Jay, and James Madison. The purpose of these essays was to gain support for the new Constitution of the United States.

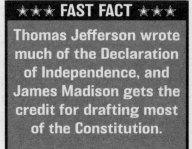

★★★ **FAST FACT** ★★★

Thomas Jefferson wrote much of the Declaration of Independence, and James Madison gets the credit for drafting most of the Constitution.

Q. When was the heralded Bill of Rights added to the Constitution?

A. December 15, 1791. During the process of ratifying the Constitution, some in the opposition expressed concern that certain basic rights were not specifically addressed. Many leaders ratified the Constitution with the understanding that the document would soon be amended to address those concerns. The Bill of Rights encompasses the first 10 amendments to the Constitution, which address rights including freedom of speech and due process.

Q. When did the White House on Pennsylvania Avenue welcome its first presidential residents?

A. November 1, 1800. The history of the White House began when President George Washington and city planner Pierre L'Enfant chose 1600 Pennsylvania Avenue as the site for the presidential residence. Irish-born architect James Hoban's design was chosen in a competition to find a builder of the "President's House." Construction began in October 1792. Although Washington oversaw the building of the house, he never lived in it. President John Adams and his wife, Abigail, moved in as the first residents on November 1, 1800.

★ The White House hasn't always been known as such. The presidential domicile has also been called the "President's Palace," the "President's House," and the "Executive Mansion." In 1901, President Theodore Roosevelt officially gave the White House its current name.

Q. What inspired Francis Scott Key to write "The Star-Spangled Banner"?

A. During the War of 1812, Francis Scott Key was a lawyer negotiating with the British for the release of an American civilian whom the British had detained on suspicion that he was responsible for the arrests of British deserters. Key was successful in his negotiations with the British, but the British detained him because they feared he would tip off the Americans about British plans to attack Baltimore. Key watched the siege of Baltimore from a British ship. Key's inspiration for "The Star-Spangled Banner" was the sight of the American flag flying over Fort McHenry the morning of September 14, 1814—signaling American victory over the British in the Battle of Baltimore.

> ★★★ FAST FACT ★★★
>
> The original name of "The Star-Spangled Banner" was "The Defense of Fort McHenry."

Q. Thomas Jefferson had the largest personal collection of books in the United States. What happened to his books?

A. After the Library of Congress lost its collection when the British burned the library during the War of 1812, Jefferson offered his personal collection to Congress to restock the library. Congress paid Jefferson $23,950 for 6,487 volumes in 1815.

Q. For how long did the Pony Express mail service between Missouri and California run?

A. The famed Pony Express ran for only 19 months during 1860 and 1861. But in that time, its riders carried nearly 35,000 pieces of mail more than 650,000 miles! Now *that's* some riding!

TRUE OR FALSE President Abraham Lincoln scribbled the Gettysburg Address on the back of an envelope as he traveled to the battleground by train.

ANSWER False. The train part is true (as Lincoln was still finalizing his words on the morning of his speech), but the rest is just a myth. Lincoln always prepared his speeches very carefully, and he knew the important opportunity that this one provided. A number of drafts of the speech have surfaced over the years, including one on executive stationery written in Lincoln's own hand.

★ Proof that you can't please all of the people all of the time: The *Chicago Times* newspaper gave Lincoln's Gettysburg Address a poor review, saying it contained "dish-watery utterances."

Q. Which glorious national park can claim the title of America's first national park?

A. Yellowstone. The sprawling park that encompasses parts of three states was officially designated on March 1, 1872—making it America's first national park.

Truly Awesome Tales

★ ★ ★ ★ ★ ★ ★ ★ ★ ★ ★ ★

The first Anglo to explore Yellowstone was John Colter, who had traveled with Lewis and Clark. Colter explored Yellowstone with a group of fur trappers in 1807. Colter's tales of Yellowstone inspired later expeditions into the area. The most notable of these later expeditions was led by geologist Ferdinand Hayden, who brought along with him photographer William Jackson and landscape artist Thomas Moran. Upon this expedition's return, citizens were dazzled by Jackson and Moran's images of the park's wonders.

Q. When did France give the Statue of Liberty to the United States?

A. October 28, 1886. France gave the Statue of Liberty to the United States to commemorate the alliance between France and the United States during the American Revolutionary War. Edouard de Laboulaye—a French politician with a fondness for the American ideals of freedom and democracy—came up with the idea for a statue, and sculptor Auguste Bartholdi turned Laboulaye's idea into the beautiful reality Americans treasure today. Bartholdi titled the statue "Liberty Enlightening the World," but it has come to commonly be called the Statue of Liberty.

⭐ During the American Revolutionary War, France initially covertly assisted the fledgling nation through ammunition and technical assistance; eventually French troops and naval power openly contributed to the American cause.

Statue of Liberty Facts

★ ★ ★ ★ ★ ★ ★ ★ ★ ★ ★ ★

1. The model for the face of the statue is reputed to be the sculptor's mother, Charlotte Bartholdi.

2. The inscription on the statue's tablet reads: July 4, 1776 (in Roman numerals).

3. The statue's hand is 16 feet 5 inches long and her index finger is 8 feet long. Her fingernails are 13 inches long by 10 inches wide and weigh about 3.5 pounds each.

4. Lady Liberty's eyes are each 2 feet 6 inches across, she has a 35-foot waistline, and she weighs about 450,000 pounds (225 tons).

5. More than 4 million people visit the Statue of Liberty each year.

Q. What significant event happened on October 9, 1936?

A. The Hoover Dam began operation on this date. Through this massive dam, Americans gained control of the mighty Colorado River, diverting its water from its natural route (the Pacific) and into Lake Mead instead. From Lake Mead, the water flows through aqueducts to farmers, ranchers, and others in the deserts of the Southwest.

★★★ **FAST FACT** ★★★

The Hoover Dam also generates the electricity that powers Southwestern cities.

Q. When did Rosa Parks take her famous stand for equality and dignity?

A. December 1, 1955. Rosa Parks was asked to give up her seat on a Montgomery, Alabama, bus to a white passenger. Parks refused and was arrested and fined. Her simple act started the civil rights movement in earnest in the United States.

> *"I did not get on the bus to get arrested.*
> *I got on the bus to go home."*
> —Rosa Parks

Q. When did Martin Luther King Jr. give his "I Have a Dream" speech?

A. August 28, 1963. King gave his speech in front of the Lincoln Memorial during the March on Washington for Jobs and Freedom.

Martin Luther King Jr.

Other March on Washington Speakers

★ ★ ★ ★ ★ ★ ★ ★ ★ ★ ★ ★

1. **Matthew Ahmann** of the National Catholic Conference for Interracial Justice
2. **Dr. Eugene Carson Blake** of the National Council of Churches
3. **James Farmer** of the Congress of Racial Equality (CORE)
4. **John Lewis** of the Student Non-Violent Coordinating Committee (SNCC)
5. **Rabbi Joachim Prinz** of the American Jewish Congress
6. **A. Philip Randolph** of the Brotherhood of Sleeping Car Porters
7. **Walter Reuther** of the United Auto Workers union
8. **Roy Wilkins** of the NAACP
9. **Whitney Young** of the National Urban League

CULTURE

★ ★ ★ ★ ★ ★ ★ ★ ★ ★ ★ ★

The culture of a nation—its day-to-day life, what it celebrates,
what it strives for—sends a unique message to the world.
Read on to refresh your memory about the defining
moments in American culture.

Q. Areas of the United States are dotted with earthen mounds.
When were these mounds built, and why?

A. Most scientists believe that some of these earthen mounds
were built as early as 3400 B.C. From studying the mounds,
scientists believe uses for the mounds varied—some served as
residences for important persons, others were used as sites for
religious services or burials.

Q. What is the oldest church in the United
States, and when was it built?

A. San Miguel Mission in Santa Fe,
New Mexico, is known as the oldest church
in the United States. It was built in 1610.

Q. On what date did the first public school in the United States
open?

A. Boston Latin School opened in 1635. It was the first
public school and is the oldest school in continuous operation
in the United States.

⭐ Horace Mann introduced age grading (assigning students to a specific grade based on age) to American schools in 1848. Before Mann's reforms, teachers had taught a mixed class of students (generally aged 6 to 14).

Q. When did the people now referred to as Cajuns settle in Louisiana?

A. Cajuns descend from the Acadians, people of French descent who had lived in Nova Scotia, New Brunswick, and Prince Edward Island before British forces defeated the French in the Seven Years' War. After this conflict came to a close in 1763, all people of French descent were exiled from these areas. Some of the Acadians traveled to Louisiana (which was under Spanish rule at the time). The term *Cajun* evolved from the word *Acadian*.

Q. When was the first American novel published?

A. 1791. William Hill Brown's *The Power of Sympathy* was the first American novel. It relates the tragic love story between siblings who unknowingly embark on an incestuous relationship. The novel was based on a real-life Boston love triangle and promoted rational thinking over giving in to one's passions.

Q. When did Hawaii's elaborate kapu system come to an end, and who ended it?

A. After the death of Kamehameha I in 1819, his son and successor Kamehameha II ended the kapu system, which was a code that strictly governed behavior in Hawaii. Kapu had been the guiding force in Hawaiian society for centuries.

★ The symbolic act that Kamehameha II performed to signal the end of the kapu system was when he sat down at the women's table on his first official appearance as king.

TRUE OR FALSE The tradition of quilting took hold in America to make use of leftover fabric scraps.

ANSWER False. It is a misconception that people made quilts just for practical purposes. In fact, most quilters engaged in quilting as a hobby because they loved the craft—not because they needed a blanket or wanted to make use of remaining scraps. By 1820, sewing groups were widespread, allowing people to work together to sew quilts that were pulled across large frames.

Q. The 1820 sinking of the *Essex* was the inspiration for which classic American novel?

A. Herman Melville's *Moby-Dick*. The *Essex* was a Nantucket whaling ship that met an untimely end in the South Pacific when an enraged sperm whale rammed and sank the 238-ton ship.

★ Melville's novel ended when the ship went down, but that was just the beginning of the story for the 20 men who survived the sperm whale's wrath in 1820. They spent months aboard three small boats and crossed more than 4,500 miles of ocean before they reached the South American coastline. Unsurprisingly, not all of the men survived the odyssey.

TRUE OR FALSE The Smithsonian Institution was the first American museum.

ANSWER False. The Charleston Museum, founded in 1773, was the first American museum. However, it did not open to the public until 1824.

Q. When and how was the esteemed Smithsonian Institution founded?

A. The idea for the Smithsonian came about when Englishman James Smithson died in 1835 and left behind an endowment for an American institution "for the increase and diffusion of knowledge among men." The first structure to be built using funds from this endowment was "the Castle"—the brownish-red stone building that comes to mind when most people think of the Smithsonian. The Castle was completed in 1855.

★ Fueled by the great American explorations of the Arctic, Antarctic, and interior regions of the United States, the Smithsonian's holdings grew from a small collection of pressed flora and preserved animal specimens to an assemblage that required the construction of a new building, the United States National Museum, in 1881.

Q. What publication sent Henry Morton Stanley in search of Dr. David Livingstone in 1871?

A. The *New York Herald.* When Stanley came upon the missionary near Lake Tanganyika in south-central Africa in 1871, he claimed to have greeted Livingstone with the words, "Dr. Livingstone, I presume?" The words have been ingrained in American culture ever since.

Q. When was JELL-O (America's best-selling prepared dessert) invented?

A. JELL-O dates back to 1845, when Peter

> ★★★ **FAST FACT** ★★★
> Approximately 300 million boxes of JELL-O are still sold every year.

Cooper obtained a patent for a flavorless gelatin dessert. Cooper packaged the product in convenient boxes—complete with instructions—but did little to promote it. In the 1890s, Pearle B. Wait perfected a fruit-flavored version of Cooper's gelatin dessert. In 1899, Wait sold the business to his neighbor, Orator Frank Woodward, owner of the Genesee Pure Food Company. A savvy promoter, Woodward began advertising JELL-O in magazines such as *Ladies' Home Journal,* calling it "America's Most Famous Dessert." Sales soared, and they have never really waned.

Q. When did progressive education begin in earnest in the United States?

A. Francis Parker spearheaded the spread of the progressive education movement in the United States between 1875 and 1880, when he served as superintendent of schools in Quincy, Massachusetts. Parker believed that schools should be concerned with the development of the child as a whole rather than simply instilling in children the capacity to perform certain calculations or memorize specific facts. The schools in Quincy stressed group activities and observation instead of standardization and rote learning. Parker thought that children coming to their own conclusions would lead to a more advanced, productive society.

> ★★★ **FAST FACT** ★★★
> Parker's Quincy experiment was considered successful after Quincy students fared better than other Massachusetts children on state-ordered tests in 1879.

Q. In 1882, President Chester Alan Arthur refused to move into the White House until it had been redecorated. Which noted American artist got the job?

A. Louis Comfort Tiffany. He worked on the East Room, the Blue Room, the Red Room, the State Dining Room, and the Entrance Hall. He had some areas repainted using decorative patterns and chose to use wallpaper with dense patterns in other rooms. He also added his signature Tiffany glass to fixtures and windows.

★★★ **FAST FACT** ★★★

The famous Tiffany & Co. jewelry company was founded by Louis Comfort Tiffany's father.

TRUE OR FALSE Upon release of the American edition of *The Adventures of Huckleberry Finn* in 1885, several libraries banned the book.

ANSWER True. Despite the antiracist tenor of the work, Mark Twain's tale of a young rascal who teams up with a runaway slave was banned upon its release in America, and it has been banned numerous times since. Nevertheless, the book reveals the hypocrisy of racism like few books before or since.

★ Samuel Clemens, aka Mark Twain, was born in 1835, the year that Halley's Comet appeared. Twain predicted that he would die on its next appearance in 1910. He was right.

Q. When did Saint Paul, Minnesota, begin holding its annual Winter Carnival?

A. 1886. The city planned the first Winter Carnival to disprove a rumor, which was started by a New York City newspaper, that Saint Paul was "another Siberia, unfit for human habitation in the winter."

TRUE OR FALSE American film pioneer Edwin S. Porter shot his groundbreaking 1903 western, *The Great Train Robbery*, in Hollywood, California.

ANSWER False. Director Edwin S. Porter shot his masterpiece entirely in West Orange, New Jersey, at Thomas Edison's studio (called the "Black Maria") and on location. Most of the earliest American films were produced in studios in New Jersey, New York, or Chicago before the industry moved to the West Coast. In fact, Hollywood didn't see its first actual movie studio until 1911.

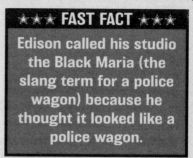

★★★ **FAST FACT** ★★★

Edison called his studio the Black Maria (the slang term for a police wagon) because he thought it looked like a police wagon.

Q. Who came up with the idea for the huggable, timeless teddy bear?

A. Morris and Rose Michtom introduced the first teddy bear in 1903. The Michtoms produced and sold stuffed bears in their small toy store in Brooklyn. They sent one of their bears to President Theodore Roosevelt and asked his permission to call it a "teddy bear" in his honor. The president liked the idea and agreed, and thankful children have been comforted ever since.

Q. When and where did the first movie theater open in the United States?

A. The first building designed specifically to show movies was The Nickelodeon in Pittsburgh. It opened in June 1905 and showed three or four one-reel films continuously throughout the day. Within three years, thousands of similar operations, called nickelodeons after the original Nickelodeon, had opened around the country.

Q. When did the first cherry blossoms bloom in the capital of Washington, D.C.?

A. Thank Helen Taft (wife of President William Howard Taft) for the beautiful cherry blossom season in the nation's capital. The idea of cherry blossoms along the Potomac originated with socialite Eliza Ruhamah Scidmore, who was dazzled by the trees during a 1885 visit to Japan. Scidmore wrote to Mrs. Taft, suggesting the trees be planted along the Potomac in Washington, D.C. The first lady liked the idea and championed it to its fulfillment. When a chemist visiting the Japanese consul in Washington heard about the plan, he and the consul pledged 3,000 trees in the name of the City of Tokyo. In March 1912, Helen Taft and the wife of the Japanese Ambassador planted the first cherry trees in Washington, D.C.

> **★★★ FAST FACT ★★★**
>
> In observance of Arbor Day in 1908, Dr. David Fairchild, an official from the U.S. Department of Agriculture, presented cherry saplings to all District of Columbia schoolchildren.

Q. What groundbreaking show introduced Cubism to American art aficionados?

A. The Armory Show of 1913. American art lovers were shocked by the Postimpressionist and Cubist works. The show moved from New York to Chicago, where students of the Art Institute burned Henri Matisse in effigy and put the artist on (a mock) trial.

TRUE OR FALSE The *New York Times* was the first newspaper to print a crossword puzzle.

ANSWER False. The first-ever crossword puzzle appeared in the *New York World* on

December 12, 1913. It was in the shape of a diamond and was designed by Arthur Wynne, who called it a "word-cross." The puzzle was an immediate hit.

Q. When did frozen food become available for purchase in the United States?

A. 1930. In 1924, while he was working as a fur trader in Labrador, Newfoundland, Canada, Clarence Birdseye noticed that the fish he caught froze almost immediately after they came out of the water. After experimenting with thawing the fish, he was excited to realize that they tasted good even after being frozen for months. Frozen vegetables, fruit, seafood, and meat were sold to the public for the first time in 1930 in Springfield, Massachusetts, under the label Birds Eye Frosted Foods.

Q. When was the Grand Ole Opry founded?

A. 1925. It began as a weekly radio program that featured traditional "country" music, including folk songs and classic mountain tunes. In 1939, the show moved to NBC radio, where it reached tens of thousands of listeners across the country. During the 1950s, the Opry was one of the nation's favorite radio programs. With every song played on the Opry stage broadcast across America, Nashville solidified its spot as the country music capital of the world.

7 Notable Grand Ole Opry Performers

★ ★ ★ ★ ★ ★ ★ ★ ★ ★ ★ ★

1. His skill with the harmonica was unrivaled, and a few lucky breaks got him gigs playing on Nashville radio shows. In 1927, those breaks helped land **Deford Bailey** a spot on the Opry—no formal audition necessary. Bailey was the first African American included in the Opry cast.

2. In 1938, **Roy Acuff** became a regular performer and emcee on the Grand Ole Opry radio program. Known as the "King of Country Music," his performance of "The Great Speckled Bird" changed the Opry forever (until then singers usually played second fiddle to the band).

3. Sarah Colley joined the Opry in 1940 and spent the next 50 years performing under the persona of brassy, hilarious mountain lady **Minnie Pearl**—wearing her trademark straw hat with the $1.98 price tag still attached.

4. **Hank Williams** joined the Opry cast in 1949. The first time he performed, the audience called him back for six encores.

5. **Johnny Cash** joined the Opry in 1956 following the success of his hit single "I Walk the Line." "The Man in Black" has places in both the Country Music Hall of Fame and the Rock and Roll Hall of Fame.

6. **Patsy Cline** made her first national television appearance in 1957, performing what would become her first hit song, "Walkin' After Midnight," on *Arthur Godfrey's Talent Scouts*. Cline achieved a lifelong dream three years later when she became a member of the Opry.

7. Her single "I'm a Honky Tonk Girl" reached number 14 on the country charts in 1960. That impressive debut earned **Loretta Lynn** her first appearance at the Opry later that very same year.

Q. When was the first "talkie" (motion picture with sound) released?

A. *The Jazz Singer*, the first talkie, was released in 1927 and starred Al Jolson.

⭐ One of the most enduring images from the silent-film era is Charlie Chaplin's "Little Tramp" wandering off into the distance at the end of Chaplin's silent films.

Q. When was the first Academy Awards ceremony held?

A. Douglas Fairbanks and William C. deMille hosted the Academy of Motion Picture Arts and Sciences awards ceremony in 1929. The event was attended by fewer than 250 people and lasted 15 minutes. *Wings* (1927) was the only silent film to win the Oscar for Best Picture until 2012, when *The Artist* took home the gold statuette.

> ★★★ **FAST FACT** ★★★
>
> William C. deMille was the older brother of Cecil B. DeMille. Cecil altered their last name because he thought it looked better on movie marquees.

Q. When did the iconic Empire State Building open to the public?

A. 1931. When it opened, it was the world's tallest structure. The crown jewel of the New York City skyline, it is considered one of the strongest examples of Art Deco architecture.

Q. What Depression-era event attracted more than 48 million Americans—each of whom paid 50 cents for entry?

A. The Chicago World's Fair, named "A Century of Progress" in celebration of the city's centennial, opened in 1933 and attracted nearly 50 million Americans, despite the Depression.

Q. When did the first drive-in movie theater open to ready audiences?

A. Richard M. Hollingshead Jr. opened the first drive-in movie theater in Camden, New Jersey, in 1933.

> *"The whole family is welcome—regardless of how noisy the children are."*
>
> —Advertisement for Hollingshead's drive-in theater

Q. When was the Iowa Writers' Workshop founded?

A. 1936. The Iowa Writers' Workshop is the nation's oldest graduate writing program.

★★★ FAST FACT ★★★

Such esteemed writers as Robert Frost, Kurt Vonnegut, and Jane Smiley honed their craft at the Iowa Writers' Workshop.

Q. When did Henry Luce first publish *Life* magazine in all its photographic glory?

A. 1936. *Life* was the first all-photographic American news magazine, and it became wildly popular.

⭐ At one point, *Life* magazine sold upward of 13.5 million copies a week.

Q. Which superhero launched the golden age of comics?

A. When Superman came on the scene in June 1938, comic books were forever changed. Written and drawn by high school pals Jerry Siegel and Joe Shuster, Superman was superbly strong and jumped one-eighth of a mile in a single bound (it would be a little while before he actually flew).

> ★★★ **FAST FACT** ★★★
>
> Cocreator Jerry Siegel said he came up with Superman on a sleepless night in the early 1930s, but it took him several years to actually sell the pitch.

Q. When did the *New York Times* first print its revered best-seller list?

A. The first weekly *New York Times* best-seller list appeared on August 9, 1942. The number-one best-selling novel was *And Now Tomorrow* by Rachel Field. It was about a doctor's search for a cure for deafness, and it held the top spot for a week.

Q. What was particularly noteworthy about Rodgers and Hammerstein's *Oklahoma!*, which opened on Broadway in 1943?

A. *Oklahoma!* was the first musical to treat music, dance, and story as an integrated unit. It ran for an unprecedented 2,000 performances and transformed American musical theater.

TRUE OR FALSE MTV's *Real World*, which was released in 1992, was the first reality TV show.

ANSWER False. Allen Funt's hidden camera show *Candid Camera*, which aired for the first time in 1948, is considered to have begun the reality genre because it involved unsuspecting ordinary people reacting to pranks.

Q. In what year did the Charles M. Schulz comic strip *Peanuts* make its debut?

A. 1950. That year, the United Feature Syndicate distributed the strip to seven newspapers.

★★★ **FAST FACT** ★★★

The United Feature Syndicate christened Schulz's comic strip *Peanuts* (Schulz had called it *L'il Folks*). Schulz never liked the new title.

Q. What was the first event televised in color from coast to coast?

A. The 1954 Tournament of Roses Parade was televised nationally in its full, multicolored glory.

★★★ **FAST FACT** ★★★

Disney World is the most visited entertainment resort in the world.

TRUE OR FALSE Walt Disney opened Disneyland before Disney World.

ANSWER True. Disneyland—Walt Disney's first amusement park—opened July 18, 1955. Disney World did not open until 1971, five years after Walt Disney's death.

Q. When was Elvis Presley's first American television appearance?

A. Elvis appeared on *The Dorsey Brothers Stage Show* on January 28, 1956—his first appearance on American television. Elvis performed two songs: "Shake, Rattle, and Roll" and "I Got a Woman."

★ In 1958, fuel company Esso warned motorists that listening to rock 'n' roll in their cars might cause a money drain. The company's researchers claimed that the beat of the music gave drivers a lead foot, thereby wasting gas.

Q. In what year was the best-selling jazz album of all time released?

A. Miles Davis's *Kind of Blue* was released in 1959. It still sells approximately 5,000 copies every week.

Q. In what year did New York City's Guggenheim Museum open?

A. 1959. Designed by celebrated architect Frank Lloyd Wright, the Guggenheim Museum houses the Guggenheim Foundation's collection of modern masterpieces. When the Guggenheim opened in 1959, visitors were invited to start at the top of the building and follow a gently sloping curve downward. Absent were the boxlike rooms so typical of the average museum. Instead, Wright's spiral of concrete drew visitors from one exhibit space to the next. The open rotunda provided a dazzling view of different paintings on several levels at once.

TRUE OR FALSE *To Kill a Mockingbird* was author Harper Lee's first book.

ANSWER True. It was also her last book, however. Published in 1960, *To Kill a Mockingbird* was the only novel Harper Lee ever published. It garnered her a Pulitzer Prize for Fiction.

Q. When the Peace Corps was established in 1961, what was its stated goal?

A. Initiated by President John F. Kennedy, the Peace Corps was founded with the intent of bringing peace to the world through volunteer service.

Q. What 1960s song inspired a dance craze of the same name?

A. Chubby Checker's number-one song "The Twist." The twist was the first modern dance style that did not require a partner, and couples who did dance together did not have to touch each other while dancing. Soon everyone was jumping on the bandwagon with a twist record: Joey Dee and The Starliters reached number one with "The Peppermint Twist," while Sam Cooke was "Twistin' the Night Away."

> *"It's like putting out a cigarette with both feet,*
> *[or] coming out of a shower and wiping your bottom*
> *with a towel to the beat of the music."*
> —Chubby Checker, explaining how to do the twist

Q. What music group invented California rock (a genre that celebrated surfing, dating, and driving)?

A. The Beach Boys, a rock 'n' roll group formed in 1961 featuring Al Jardine, Mike Love, and the three Wilson brothers (Brian, Carl, and Dennis) invented California rock. The group, which was noted for its rich harmonies and thoughtful lyrics, helped change

★★★ **FAST FACT** ★★★
Of all The Beach Boys, Dennis was the only one who actually surfed.

the landscape of modern rock 'n' roll. The sound and lyrics of The Beach Boys made every day seem like a romp in the surf.

Q. Which summer is wistfully remembered as the "Summer of Love"?

A. The summer of 1967, which featured the Monterey Pop Festival, is remembered as the Summer of Love. In the face of the Vietnam War, a counterculture emerged that preached love, not war as a means to solve the problems of the world.

Q. When did the countdown show *American Top 40* hit the airwaves?

A. July 4, 1970. Casey Kasem hosted the show from its inception up until 1988, then again from 1998 until 2004, when Ryan Seacrest took over.

Q. When did the first successful video game system go on the market?

A. 1977. Atari 2600, created by Nolan Bushnell and Ted Dabney, was the first successful home video game system.

TRUE OR FALSE *Gunsmoke* holds the record for the longest-running scripted American primetime television series.

ANSWER False. *The Simpsons* took this record over from *Gunsmoke* in 2009.

STRUGGLES AND CONFLICTS

★ ★ ★ ★ ★ ★ ★ ★ ★ ★ ★ ★

The history of any great nation is peppered with struggles, and the United States has not escaped such trials.

Q. When was the first significant conflict between the colonists and the Native Americans?

A. King Philip's War, which lasted from 1675 to 1676. This conflict arose chiefly over land; the Native Americans began to feel threatened by the colonists, who seemed to need more land by the minute. After Wampanoag chief Metacomet (who also went by the European name Philip, which led the colonists to nickname him "King Philip") rose to power, the Wampanoag began randomly attacking colonial settlements. The colonists demanded the Wampanoag surrender their arms; the Wampanoag complied, but after John Sassamon, a Native American who was working for the colonists, was murdered, tensions mounted further. The colonists arrested and hung three Wampanoag, an action the Wampanoag viewed as an unnecessary display of force. The Wampanoag retaliated by attacking colonial villages. The colonists eventually succeeded in killing King Philip, which ended the war.

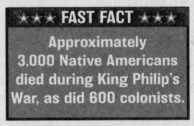

★ ★ ★ **FAST FACT** ★ ★ ★

Approximately 3,000 Native Americans died during King Philip's War, as did 600 colonists.

Q. Where were the first shots of the Revolutionary War fired?

A. The original shots "heard 'round the world" were fired at Lexington and Concord in Massachusetts on April 19, 1775.

TRUE OR FALSE Most of the fighting in the first major battle of the Revolutionary War took place on Breed's Hill in Boston.

ANSWER True. This battle in June 1775 was for control of two hills overlooking Boston Harbor: Bunker Hill and Breed's Hill. Though the battle came to popularly be called the Battle of Bunker Hill, most of the fighting took place on Breed's Hill. The Americans, led by Colonel William Prescott, had built a defensive enclosure on top of Breed's Hill. It took the British three tries before they captured the hill. That capture came at a high price—of 2,200 British soldiers, almost half were killed or wounded.

Colonel William Prescott

"Don't one of you fire until you see the whites of their eyes!"

—American Colonel William Prescott, to colonial soldiers
(Prescott was attempting to conserve dwindling ammunition stores)

Q. What do the dates September 19, 1777, and October 7, 1777, have in common?

A. They're both dates for the Battle of Saratoga. On September 19, British General John Burgoyne's forces collided with American troops and successfully beat them back, but not without taking heavy casualties. Thus, when the Americans attacked again on October 7, Burgoyne surrendered—marking a crucial American victory that turned the tide of the Revolutionary War.

Q. What break rejuvenated patriot troops for the closing sessions of the war?

A. Valley Forge. Following defeats at Brandywine and Germantown, George Washington led his troops to winter quarters at Valley Forge. The session the troops spent at Valley Forge helped them form a stronger bond with their leader, Washington, who stayed

Valley Forge, soldier's cabin

with them through this stretch. It also gave Baron Friedrich Wilhelm von Steuben time to train and drill the troops. When spring came, the troops were also greeted with the good news that France would be openly offering its support and aid. The troops came out of Valley Forge renewed and with firm resolve.

TRUE OR FALSE At times, Americans wavered in their support and confidence in General Washington.

ANSWER True. Leading up to the winter session at Valley Forge, Congress was beginning to have its doubts about General Washington. However, after the troops emerged from Valley Forge and were victorious at Monmouth, any murmurings about replacing Washington were silenced.

> *"...we must not, in so great a contest, expect to meet with nothing but Sun shine."*
> —General George Washington

Q. At what Virginia location did British General Cornwallis's surrender take place?

A. Yorktown. The Battle of Yorktown ended on October 19, 1781. Yorktown was the last significant battle of the war and one that the Continental army probably would not have won without help from France. Roughly 9,000 French soldiers and 15,000 French sailors joined about 11,000 Americans to surround a much smaller British force. General Charles Cornwallis's loss broke Britain's will to continue fighting, and the English Crown entered negotiations to end the war. It took nearly two years before the Treaty of Paris was signed, which marked the official cessation of hostilities. Twenty-two days after the signing of the treaty, British troops left America.

Q. More than 60 soldiers, women, and children were massacred in 1812 during what event?

A. The Fort Dearborn Massacre. During the War of 1812, the Americans believed that British troops and their Native American allies would soon be attacking Fort Dearborn. U.S. General William Hull sent word to Captain Heald (who was in charge of Fort

Fort Dearborn

Dearborn) to evacuate the fort. Unfortunately, Heald did not immediately follow the command, which gave the Potawatomi time to surround the fort. Heald made an agreement with the Potawatomi: He and his people would be allowed to leave the fort unharmed if they left all their extra provisions, including ammunition and weapons, inside the fort. Some fort residents—

Fort Dearborn

★ ★ ★ ★ ★ ★ ★ ★ ★ ★ ★ ★

Fort Dearborn, which was situated near the current intersection of Wacker Drive and Michigan Avenue in Chicago, was a major strategic site because of its access to waterways, trails, and forests. The fort had few residents until 1810, when Captain Heald was put in charge of a small garrison due to rising conflict with the British. When the War of 1812 began in earnest, there were approximately 100 men, women, and children living at the fort.

In July 1812 the garrison on Michigan's Mackinac Island was captured by the British army. Shortly thereafter, many Native Americans began joining with the British forces to attack U.S. forts and outposts. It quickly became clear to the U.S. forces that the Brits' next stop would be Fort Dearborn.

concerned that any weapons left behind might be used against them—disposed of the guns and ammunition in an abandoned well. Potawatomi scouts observed the residents doing this, and the Potawatomi became furious. When the residents evacuated on August 15, 1812, the Potawatomi turned on them. By the time the massacre ended, most of the 100 people who had left the fort had been killed.

Q. On August 24, 1814, the White House burned to the ground. Why?

A. When the British defeated the Americans at the Battle of Bladensburg during the War of 1812, they celebrated

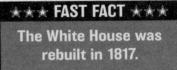

★★★ **FAST FACT** ★★★

The White House was rebuilt in 1817.

their victory by setting fire to Washington, D.C. Many revered American buildings were destroyed. Only the stone skeleton of the White House survived.

Q. What did the Missouri Compromise stipulate?

A. The Missouri Compromise, enacted in 1820, stipulated that Missouri would join the Union as a slave state, Maine would join as a free state, and slavery would be banned in the remaining Louisiana Purchase territory north of 36°30′.

"**Infernal Machine,**" found at Washington.

S. C. Upham, 310 Chestnut St.

Q. What was the Trail of Tears?

A. In 1830, Congress passed the Indian Removal Act. Using that act in 1838, President Andrew Jackson sent troops to Georgia, Tennessee, North Carolina, and Alabama to resettle the Cherokee west of the Mississippi River. More than 4,000 Cherokee died during the journey.

★★★ **FAST FACT** ★★★

One reason for the removal of the Native Americans was the discovery of gold in Cherokee territory.

Q. When did the Mormons settle in Utah?

A. After founder Joseph Smith was murdered by a mob in Illinois in 1844, the Mormons fled west. In 1847, they arrived in the area that is now Utah. Under Brigham Young's leadership, pioneer settlements of Mormons prospered as far north as the Oregon territory and as far west as the Pacific.

★★★ **FAST FACT** ★★★

Utah became a state in 1896.

A Wandering People

★ ★ ★ ★ ★ ★ ★ ★ ★ ★ ★ ★

After founding the Mormon Church in 1830, Joseph Smith searched for a peaceful place to settle down with his followers. Wherever they went, trouble followed, however. They first settled in Kirtland, Ohio, but residents there soon grew resentful of the newcomers. Smith and his followers next moved to Far West, Missouri. Their new neighbors soon rose up against them, and the Mormons moved to Commerce, Illinois, and renamed the town Nauvoo (Hebrew for "beautiful place"). This settlement was peaceful for several years, but then the group again eventually aroused resentment from neighboring communities.

Smith served as mayor and chief judge in Nauvoo, and when a community newspaper published an article critical of the Mormons, Smith ordered the newspaper's office shut down. This action sparked riots. Authorities from nearby Carthage arrested Smith and charged him with inciting a riot. On June 27, 1844, a large mob attacked Smith at the Carthage jail. Smith was shot multiple times and died as he tried to escape through a second-story window.

Q. When did Santa Anna and his men attack the Alamo?

A. Originally a Franciscan mission in San Antonio, the Alamo was used as a fort in the Texan fight against Mexico. In February 1836, General Antonio López de Santa Anna led 2,000 Mexican soldiers against the 150 Texans at the Alamo. The siege lasted into March, when the remaining warriors fought hand-to-hand with Mexican troops inside the garrison. All 150 Texans were killed, along with 600 Mexican soldiers.

★★★ **FAST FACT** ★★★

The cry "Remember the Alamo!" helped defeat Santa Anna later at the Battle of San Jacinto.

Q. When did the Mexican army announce that they would be taking no prisoners at the Alamo?

A. February 23, 1836. The Mexicans raised a dark red flag on the Alamo side of the San Fernando Church when they arrived. The red flag, symbolic of the blood that would be spilled, signified to the Texan forces that they would receive no mercy.

Q. How long was Davy Crockett at the Alamo?

A. Davy Crockett was at the Alamo for just shy of one month. He arrived on February 8, 1836, and brought with him 12 volunteers. Though he fought passionately to defend the stronghold from General Santa Anna's forces, he was among those who gave their lives in the battle. He died there on March 6, 1836—the day the battle ended.

TRUE OR FALSE Daniel Boone did not fight at the Alamo.

ANSWER True. Boone, born in 1734, died 16 years before the Battle of the Alamo.

★ Daniel Boone helped blaze the Cumberland Gap trail from Virginia into Kentucky and Tennessee.

Q. When were the first impeachment proceedings of a U.S. president?

A. 1842. John Tyler became president after the sudden death of William Henry Harrison. Tyler's policies made him unpopular. After being expelled from the Whig party and having all but one member of his cabinet resign, the House of Representatives began impeachment proceedings when Tyler vetoed a tariff bill. The impeachment resolution ultimately failed, and Tyler stayed in office.

Q. When did the Donner party set out, and where were they headed?

A. In the spring of 1846, George Donner formed a group of 86 people to head west from Independence, Missouri, to Sutter's Fort in California. They believed it was their "manifest destiny" to claim territory out west and seek their fortunes.

Q. What happened to impede the Donner party's arrival at its destination?

A. When the Donner party came upon the Little Sandy River (in present-day Wyoming), they made the fatal mistake of attempting a shortcut George Donner knew about from reading Lansford Hastings's *The Emigrant's Guide to Oregon and California*. The "shortcut" ended up putting them three weeks behind schedule. By then, many travelers had fallen ill. In the middle of October, the group got stuck in a blizzard in the mountains—more than 100 miles from its destination.

Q. Did the Donner party ever make it to California?

A. Two-thirds of the men and one-third of the women and children died on the journey. When the food ran out, the

Sutter's Fort, Sacramento, California

oxen were slaughtered and eaten. A few members set out to find help (the rest of the party was too weak to travel). The rescue group found help in California and was able to return and guide half of the Donner party to California. The rest were too weak to begin the trip and had to wait for a second rescue team. Some of the remaining members resorted to cannibalism in order to make it through the winter. The 45 survivors reached Sutter's Fort more than a year after the party had left Missouri.

Q. The statehood of California and Texas and the creation of the New Mexico and Utah Territories were due to what famous piece of legislation?

A. The Compromise of 1850. The borders that were redefined satisfied both Northerners and Southerners, but while the Compromise addressed slavery, it avoided taking a firm stance. The legislation postponed civil war for another ten years.

TRUE OR FALSE Virginia was the first state to secede from the Union.

ANSWER False. South Carolina was the first state to secede, and it did so on December 20, 1860.

★ Ten more states seceded in 1861. The 11 states established the Confederate States of America.

Q. Why was the Battle of Bull Run called a "picnic battle"?

A. It was supposed to be a walk in the park for Union forces. They were to put down the Confederate rebellion in

★★★ **FAST FACT** ★★★

The Union defeat at Bull Run proved to the spectators that the Civil War would not be a short one.

a quick effort and then march back to Washington as heroes. On July 16, 1861, General Irvin McDowell marched his untrained force out of Washington. The soldiers were having a grand time. Washingtonians didn't

Battlefield at Bull Run

want to miss the excitement of the battle either, so many followed on horseback or in buggies loaded down with picnic baskets. The battle took place on July 21, 1861.

Q. When was the first time that a railroad was used to mobilize troops for a strategic advantage?

A. On July 18, 1861, Confederate General Joseph E. Johnston moved his troops from Winchester to Manassas via the Manassas Gap Railroad for the First Battle of Bull Run.

TRUE OR FALSE Only male soldiers took part in the Battle of Bull Run.

ANSWER False. Kady Brownell, a soldier's daughter and wife of a 6th Rhode Island infantryman, followed her husband into battle and fought side by side with him at the First Battle of Bull Run. She tended the

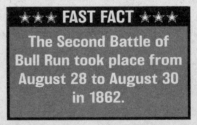
★★★ **FAST FACT** ★★★
The Second Battle of Bull Run took place from August 28 to August 30 in 1862.

wounded, and when the regiment's standard-bearer was hit, she picked it up and carried it into combat.

Q. On what date did the U.S. Navy's USS *Monitor* face the Confederacy's CSS *Virginia*?

A. March 9, 1862. Although both sides worked on their own ironclad ships simultaneously, the North and South came up with radically different designs. The CSS *Virginia* was partially made from the hull of the Northern frigate USS *Merrimack*. This impressive vessel had 2-inch plates mounted on the 24-foot-high sides of the ship. On the other side, the *Monitor* rode exceedingly low in the water, with only the 9-foot-tall turret visible above the waterline. The ships fought to a stalemate in history's first battle of ironclad gunboats. The two vessels served as prototypes for the modern warships that were used in the two world wars.

Q. Which battle turned the tide of the Civil War toward the Union?

A. The Battle of Shiloh (also known as the Battle of Pittsburg Landing). Confederate Generals Albert Sidney Johnston and P. G. T. Beauregard launched a surprise attack against General Grant and nearly defeated him. Fought in April 1862, Shiloh was the bloodiest battle in American history up to that time. It was the Confederates' last stand to prevent a Union invasion of Mississippi.

Q. How did breakfast figure in the Battle of Shiloh?

A. Confederate General Albert Sidney Johnston's forces surprised the Union soldiers on April 6, 1862. With the Union army on the run, the Confederates' stomachs betrayed them. The federal soldiers had been making breakfast, and in the rush of battle, they left the food behind. Some of the rebels slowed their attack to gobble down a meal, giving Grant's army a chance to pull together. The next day, Union General Don Carlos Buell arrived with his forces and retook the ground the Union had lost the day before.

Q. Abraham Lincoln issued the Emancipation Proclamation after which Civil War battle?

A. Antietam. Although technically a draw, Lincoln was impressed enough with the strength of the Union army— which forced Southern forces to retreat back across the Potomac on September 17, 1862—that he decided it was time to issue this important proclamation.

TRUE OR FALSE The Emancipation Proclamation freed every slave in America.

ANSWER False. The language of the document was clear: Any slave that was still held in the states that had seceded from the Union was "forever free" as of January 1, 1863. Significantly, this edict did not include border states in which slaves were still held, such as Kentucky or Missouri, because Lincoln didn't want to stoke rebellion there. As one might expect, the Southern states paid little heed to the announcement by the Union president. They'd already turned their backs on him and his nation, and as far as they were concerned, the Union president held no power over them.

Q. Which Civil War battle is known as Robert E. Lee's "perfect battle"?

A. Chancellorsville. General Lee surveyed the situation in early May 1863 and made the risky decision to divide

★★★ FAST FACT ★★★

Confederate General Stonewall Jackson was mortally wounded by friendly fire at the Battle of Chancellorsville.

his army in the face of a much larger Union force. The battle played out much as Lee predicted (with the victory going to the Confederates)—thus Chancellorsville is known as Lee's perfect battle.

Q. How long did the Siege of Vicksburg last, and when did it end?

A. The Union army surrounded Vicksburg in May 1863, bombing it and hoping to starve out the Confederates and citizenry alike. Civilians found only one way to escape the bombardment—move underground. They took advantage of the rolling hills and dug caves into the bluffs and hillsides. Vicksburg surrendered to General Grant on July 4, 1863—day 47 of the siege and the day after General Lee was defeated at Gettysburg. When the citizens crawled out of their caves, they found Vicksburg a pile of rubble. The shelling had destroyed everything. The defeat was so traumatic to the town, it did not celebrate Independence Day again for 82 years.

> **★★★ FAST FACT ★★★**
>
> **The Union victory at Vicksburg split the Confederacy in two.**

Q. When did angry draftees demonstrate just how much they didn't want to join the army during the Civil War?

A. July 13 through July 16, 1863. On Sunday, July 12, 1863, New York newspapers printed the names of those who had been drafted the day before. The next morning, groups of people gathered to protest, peaceably at first. Rioters yelled racial slurs, attacked and lynched free African Americans, and

> **★★★ FAST FACT ★★★**
>
> **Historians believe that the draft riots took on a racial tone because some New York residents resented being drafted into a war over slavery.**

burned the Colored Orphan Asylum as well as mixed-race broth-els and saloons. The homes of several prominent Republicans were destroyed, as was a Brooks Brothers shop that made Union army uniforms.

Q. The "War Between the States" raged on for four years, from 1861 to 1865. Once it was all over, how much had the war cost both sides, in dollars?

A. About $8.3 billion. In 1879, the gov-ernment estimated that Union army costs totaled nearly $6.2 billion. For its part, the Confederacy spent more than $2.1 billion. By 1906, another $3.3 billion was spent by the U.S. government on pensions and other veterans' benefits for former Union soldiers. Southern states and private philanthropy provided benefits to Confederate veterans.

Q. Who led a famous charge on the last day of the Battle of Gettysburg?

A. General George Pickett. In what would go down in history as Pickett's Charge, the forces of Confederate General George Pickett led the march up Cemetery Ridge in

> ★ ★ ★ **FAST FACT** ★ ★ ★
>
> James Tilton Pickett, General George Pickett's son by Morning Mist, his second wife, was a noted landscape painter in the Northwest.

1863. Nearly 12,000 soldiers marched more than a mile under heavy fire, and some managed to break through the Union line. However, lacking support behind and facing intense Union bom-bardment, they could not hold their ground; they retreated, hav-ing suffered horrific losses.

> *"I was ordered to take a height, which I did, under the most withering fire I have ever known..."*
>
> —General George Pickett, in a letter to his wife after his ill-fated charge

TRUE OR FALSE North Carolina is the only state to form by seceding from a Confederate state.

ANSWER False. West Virginia is the only state to form by seceding from a Confederate state (Virginia, in 1863). North Carolina and South Carolina became separate entities in 1712, during colonial times.

Q. How was General Custer defeated at the Battle of Little Bighorn (also known as Custer's Last Stand)?

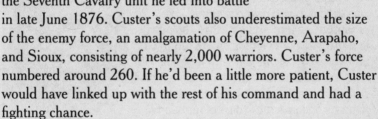

A. It was mostly Custer's impatience and arrogance that caused the massacre of the Seventh Cavalry unit he led into battle in late June 1876. Custer's scouts also underestimated the size of the enemy force, an amalgamation of Cheyenne, Arapaho, and Sioux, consisting of nearly 2,000 warriors. Custer's force numbered around 260. If he'd been a little more patient, Custer would have linked up with the rest of his command and had a fighting chance.

Q. When did Clara Barton found the American Red Cross?

A. 1881. Proof that some good can come of struggles, the founding of the American Red Cross can be traced to Clara Barton's humanitarian works during the Civil War. Cutting through official red tape, Barton won permission from the War Department to go out into the field and help the wounded. She began personally delivering critical supplies to battlefields where they were most needed. After the war, Barton traveled to Europe and was inspired by humanitarian efforts she witnessed there. Barton founded the American Red Cross upon her return to the United States in 1881.

Q. When did Jane Addams found Hull House?

A. 1889. Like Clara Barton, Jane Addams found inspiration while traveling in Europe. After finishing a stint volunteering at London's Toynbee Hall (a settlement house), Addams returned to her native Chicago to start her own settlement house.

Hull House

★ ★ ★ ★ ★ ★ ★ ★ ★ ★ ★ ★

When Addams arrived on Chicago's Near West Side, the crowded area was teeming with poverty, crime, and prostitution. Numerous brothels, saloons, and drug dealers victimized the refugees and immigrants who came to America with little money and were often unable to speak English. It was to these people that Jane Addams became the "voice of humanity."

Jane Addams

Impressed by Jane's plans for a settlement house, Helen Culver, niece of businessman Charles Hull, offered the Hull mansion to Addams with a rent-free lease. Addams converted the mansion into a safe and comfortable place that offered food, shelter, and education for the impoverished. As the operation increased in popularity, 12 more buildings were added, until eventually Hull House spread out over an entire city block. Hull House closed in 2012.

⭐ Jane Addams was a significant force on the Near West Side for decades. For instance, when she was unsatisfied with garbage collection efforts in her neighborhood, she asked the city if she could collect the garbage herself. The city declined that request but did give her the job of garbage inspector. As inspector, Addams made sure all the bins in her neighborhood were emptied in a timely fashion.

Q. When was the last significant conflict between Native Americans and the American military?

A. December 29, 1890. Lakota Sioux had been gathering for Ghost Dance rituals under Paiute prophet Wovoka in an attempt to resurrect their way of life. The U.S. government became concerned about the intent of these rituals and worked to discourage them. After Sitting Bull was killed during his arrest, tensions rose. In an ill-advised attempt to disarm the Lakota, a group of 500 men under the command of Colonel James W. Forsyth slaughtered 153 Lakota men, women, and children and injured 51 more at Wounded Knee in South Dakota. Though the civilian response at the time was supportive of the federal troops, the clash at Wounded Knee would later be dubbed a massacre after witness reports became public.

Q. In 1932 a group called the "Bonus Army" or "Bonus Expeditionary Force" converged on Washington, D.C. What did this group demand?

A. The Bonus Army, made up of 12,000 to 15,000 unemployed veterans, demanded immediate bonus payments for their World War I service. Congress had voted for the bonuses (which were to be one dollar for every day served) in 1924, but payment was not scheduled until 1945. The Bonus Army wanted the bonuses immediately to ease their suffering dur-

(Continued on page 63)

Notable Native Americans

★ ★ ★ ★ ★ ★ ★ ★ ★ ★ ★ ★

1. The principal chief of the Lakota Sioux, **Sitting Bull** was less than forgiving when white miners tried to take over the Black Hills in the late 1870s. Sitting Bull and his men defeated Custer's troops at the Battle of the Little Bighorn.

2. In 1809, when the Treaty of Fort Wayne signed over 2.5 million acres to the United States, **Tecumseh,** a Shawnee chief, was outraged. He tried to get all the Native American nations to join together, but the idea came too late.

3. Thanks to **Sequoyah,** a Cherokee born around 1766, the Cherokee language is not a mystery. Sequoyah created the syllabary, or syllable alphabet, for his people and taught the Cherokee how to read and write. The giant sequoia tree is named for the man who believed that the pen would outlast the sword.

4. Though only one-eighth Cherokee, **John Ross** served as a chief from 1828 until his death in 1866. He was president of the Cherokee Constitutional Convention of 1827 and worked for justice for the Cherokee. Even though several court rulings found the Cherokee to be the rightful owners of land, the rulings weren't enforced, and Ross's efforts went largely unrewarded. Ross led the Cherokee along the "Trail of Tears."

5. The Lakota warrior **Crazy Horse** spent his life fighting for the preservation of his people's way of life. He amassed more than 1,200 warriors to help Sitting Bull defeat General Crook in 1876.

6. For most of his life, **Red Cloud** was fighting. At first, it was to defend his Oglala people against the Pawnee and Crow, but by the time he reached his forties, Red Cloud was fighting the white man. His efforts led to victory at Fort Phil Kearny in Wyoming in 1867. In the two years that followed, the government signed the Fort Laramie Treaty and gave the Native Americans land in Wyoming, Montana, and South Dakota. But soon after, the Black Hills were invaded, and Red Cloud and his people lost their land.

(Continued from page 61)

ing the Depression. They
camped in tents along the
Anacostia River to wait for
their bonuses. When Congress
defeated a bill to speed up the

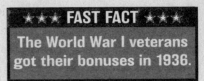

★★★ **FAST FACT** ★★★
The World War I veterans
got their bonuses in 1936.

bonuses, near-riots ensued, and Army troops, led by General
Douglas MacArthur, forced the vets off the land with tear gas.
MacArthur and his men even followed the vets across the bridge
to their encampment, ignoring President Hoover's order that this
step not be taken. In the confusion, a fire broke out at the vets'
encampment, and the veterans were forced to disperse entirely.

Q. When was the first peacetime draft established in U.S.
history?

A. 1940. The Selective Service Act established the first
peacetime draft in U.S. history in anticipation of threats
from Europe.

Q. The attack on Pearl Harbor,
which prompted the United
States to immediately join the
Allied efforts in World War II,
occurred on what day?

Bombing of Pearl Harbor

A. The Japanese attack on U.S.
naval forces at Pearl Harbor
began at 7:53 A.M. Hawaiian
time, December 7, 1941. The larg-
est loss of life at Pearl Harbor occurred when the forward magazine on the battleship USS *Arizona* exploded.

Q. What was rationed during World War II after Japan invaded
the Dutch East Indies?

A. Gasoline. It was actually rationed to keep citizens from going through automobile tires too quickly, as the Japanese invasion of the Dutch East Indies (modern Indonesia) had affected the supply of rubber.

Q. What revolutionary legislation did President Roosevelt sign on June 22, 1944?

A. The G.I. Bill. This bill provided education and one year of unemployment compensation for returning World War II veterans. Veterans were also able to obtain low-interest loans and move into suburban homes with no down payments.

Q. Joseph McCarthy's anticommunist pursuits, also known as McCarthyism, dominated American politics in what era?

> ★★★ **FAST FACT** ★★★
> The first Red Scare followed the Bolshevik Revolution in Russia and lasted from 1919 to 1920.

A. The second Red Scare lasted from the late 1940s to the late 1950s. Perhaps grasping for a campaign issue, McCarthy made the shocking claim that he had a list of 205 government officials who were communists. The Senate opened hearings on McCarthy's allegations in March 1950, but McCarthy never proved his case.

★ Many Americans believe Joe McCarthy chaired the House Un-American Activities Committee (HUAC), but McCarthy, a U.S. Senator, had no involvement with the House committee.

CIVIL RIGHTS

★ ★ ★ ★ ★ ★ ★ ★ ★ ★ ★

Sadly, the history of civil rights in the United States is similar to the history of many other areas of the globe in this regard: many steps backward before (finally) some steps forward.

Q. When did slavery begin in the American colonies?

A. Dutch traders brought the first African slaves to the Jamestown colony in 1619. Prior to that, indentured servants had been brought from England to work for seven years, after which they were granted freedom. The colonists considered that loss of labor too costly, and slavery began.

★ A historical record from 1640 indicates that a court in the colonies ruled that one particular African was to "serve his said master or his assigns for the time of his natural life here or elsewhere."

TRUE OR FALSE Women in the state of New Jersey had the right to vote in 1776.

ANSWER True. The 1776 New Jersey constitution said that, regardless of gender, "all inhabitants" with 50 pounds to their name could vote. Many women did not exercise the right until a hotly contested election in 1797, when 75 women came en masse to vote for their preferred candidate. Their candidate triumphed, and after that candidates started taking groups of women to the polls. In one 1807 election both sides battled to get women to the polls. There were even reports of boys arriving to the polls wearing women's clothing. Later that year, New Jersey lawmakers barred women from voting.

Q. When was the first Fugitive Slave Act passed?

A. 1793. It authorized the seizure of fugitives and established a $500 fine for aiding a runaway.

Q. More than 70 enslaved and free blacks killed more than 50 white men, women, and children during a slave uprising on what date?

A. August 21–22, 1831. The uprising came to be known as Nat Turner's slave rebellion. Turner, a deeply religious slave, experienced what he interpreted as visions from God his entire life, and after a series of visions, he led a group of more than 70 participants in a bloody rebellion against slavery. At least 100 blacks were killed after the rebellion, and Turner was executed on November 11, 1831.

Q. What was America's first interracial college?

A. Ohio's Oberlin College was founded in 1833 by a Presbyterian minister, the Rev. John J. Shipherd, and a missionary, Philo P. Stewart. Beginning in 1835, the school began accepting people of color. The Rev. John Keep, a trustee of the college and an abolitionist, cast the deciding vote to allow African Americans to study there. Though the school was coeducational from the beginning, women first began studying for baccalaureate degrees in 1837.

TRUE OR FALSE The Liberty Bell received its name as a symbol for the freedom of black slaves.

ANSWER True. The same bell hung in the Philadelphia State House from the time when Pennsylvania was still an English colony, but it had never been given any particular name. For some of the time it wasn't even considered significant—in 1828, for instance, Philadelphia tried to sell it for scrap, but there were no takers. The first time anyone called it the Liberty Bell was in a book by that same name distributed at the Massachusetts Anti-Slavery Fair in 1839.

Q. When did Harriet Tubman escape slavery?

A. Harriet Tubman was born around 1821 on a slave-breeding plantation in Maryland. After the master of the plantation died in 1849, it was rumored that the slaves were to be sent to the Deep South. Fearing the deadly consequences of that move, Harriet and two of her brothers decided to escape. The brothers, fearful of being apprehended, turned back, but Harriet kept walking to freedom. She eventually returned to retrieve three brothers (she had 10 siblings) and her mother and father.

Harriet Tubman

Q. When did the U.S. Supreme Court issue the infamous Dred Scott decision?

A. March 6, 1857. Dred Scott was a slave who sued to gain his freedom. He first pursued the cause in 1846, and after numerous appeals, the Supreme Court decided against him in

1857. In *Dred Scott v. Sanford,* the Supreme Court ruled that neither free nor enslaved African Americans could become U.S. citizens. The ruling also made slavery legal in all U.S. territories.

Q. Why was John Brown hanged?

A. John Brown, a passionate abolitionist, was convicted of treason against the Commonwealth of Virginia for a raid he and his followers executed on the federal arsenal at Harpers Ferry on October 16, 1859. They planned to capture weapons and then attack slaveholders and set slaves free. Brown's group took about 60 townspeople hostage, but the following day federal troops, led by Colonel Robert E. Lee, captured Brown.

Q. When did the last slave ship arrive in the United States?

A. 1859. Beginning in 1808, it was technically illegal to bring slaves from Africa into the United States; this law was often violated, however. The last recorded case of a slave ship entering the United States was in 1859, when the *Clotilde* docked in Mobile, Alabama, with more than 100 slaves from an area of western Africa near present-day Benin. More than 30 of the slaves escaped and established the settlement Africatown in southern Alabama, where they practiced the customs of their homeland.

⭐ Africatown is now part of Pritchard, Alabama (a suburb of Mobile). More than 12,000 people live in Africatown today, and many of these residents can trace their roots back to the original Africatown settlers.

Q. Who embarked on her civil rights crusade after she was dismissed from a first-class train car because she was black (even though she had paid for a first-class ticket)?

Ida B. Wells

A. Ida B. Wells. Born in Mississippi in 1862, Wells attended Rust College and went on to teach in Memphis, Tennessee. While in Memphis she served as the editor of the African American newspaper *The Free Speech and Headlight.* Her fiery editorials about the poor schools and violence against African Americans led to her dismissal from her teaching position, and she became a full-time journalist.

Q. In what year did Booker T. Washington helped found the Tuskegee Institute?

A. 1881. Born a slave in Virginia in 1856, Washington was educated at the Hampton Institute. His progress impressed the Hampton principal, who recommended Washington to a group in Alabama that was working to open a school for African Americans. Washington ran Tuskegee until his death in 1915.

⭐ The idea for the Tuskegee Institute was formed by former slave Lewis Adams, who made a deal with Alabama Senate candidate W. F. Foster to deliver the African American vote in exchange for the founding of a school for African Americans.

Q. What was the first major law restricting immigration to the United States?

A. The Chinese Exclusion Act of 1882. This law was passed because citizens on the West Coast blamed Chinese immigrants for rising unemployment and falling wages. The Chinese Exclusion Act halted Chinese immigration for a decade and prevented any Chinese from becoming citizens. Large-scale Chinese immigration did not resume until the Immigration Act of 1965.

> ★★★ **FAST FACT** ★★★
>
> Chinese immigrants helped build the Transcontinental Railroad in the 1860s.

Q. Why did W. E. B. DuBois organize a meeting in Niagara in 1905?

A. He had grown impatient with the pace of civil rights progress under Booker T. Washington's leadership. DuBois called his movement the Niagara Movement because the first meeting of the group was held near Niagara Falls. The Niagara Movement demanded equal protection under the law and the recognition and implementation of African American voting rights.

Q. Mary White Ovington held the initial meeting of the fledgling NAACP on what date in 1909 (a president's birthday)?

A. February 12. In 1908, William English Walling wrote an article decrying the fact that a terrible race riot had occurred that year in Springfield, Illinois—the birthplace of Abraham Lincoln. Walling concluded the article by remarking that it seemed that a new, powerful organization was needed to address racial issues in the country. After reading Walling's article, Mary

> ★★★ **FAST FACT** ★★★
>
> Ida Wells and W. E. B. DuBois were two of the founding members of the NAACP.

White Ovington contacted Walling, and the two—together with social worker Henry Moskovitz—issued a call for a meeting to be held on February 12, 1909 (the centennial of Abraham Lincoln's birth), to create the new organization. The document drafted at the February 12 meeting was signed by 60 prominent activists, black and white, including members of the Niagara Movement.

Q. Which Supreme Court decision established the "separate but equal" doctrine?

A. *Plessy v. Ferguson.* In 1892, Homer Plessy (who traced some of his ancestors

> ★★★ **FAST FACT** ★★★
>
> The 14th Amendment is cited at trial more often than any other amendment.

back to the French, Spanish, and Caribbean settlers of Louisiana and was therefore considered "colored") sat in the "white" car of the East Louisiana Railroad. He was arrested for doing so. Plessy's case went all the way to the U.S. Supreme Court, where his lawyers maintained that the requirement to sit in a "colored" car violated Plessy's rights under the 13th and 14th Amendments. The Supreme Court upheld Louisiana's segregation statute.

The 13th and 14th Amendments
★ ★ ★ ★ ★ ★ ★ ★ ★ ★ ★ ★

- The 13th Amendment was ratified December 6, 1885. It abolished slavery.

- The 14th Amendment was ratified July 9, 1868, and granted citizenship to "all persons born or naturalized in the United States," which included former slaves recently freed. It forbade states from denying any person "life, liberty or property, without due process of law." It also forbade states from denying any person within their jurisdictions "the equal protection of any laws."

Q. What parade held on August 3, 1920, is remembered as one of the largest in New York history?

A. Marcus Garvey's Universal Negro Improvement Association parade. Garvey was a flamboyant character whose speeches and dramatic leadership called upon African Americans to take pride in their heritage.

⭐ Garvey advocated a back-to-Africa plan that was rather controversial. From Garvey's life experience, however, he was not optimistic about African Americans ever truly being accepted into the majority-white American population.

Q. Whose rendition of the haunting anti-lynching song "Strange Fruit" thrust her onto the national stage in 1939?

A. Billie Holiday. Holiday was born in Baltimore in 1915 and had a difficult childhood. As a teen she tried to audition to be a dancer at a Harlem speakeasy, but because there was not an opening for a dancer, she tried out as a singer instead. The owner was impressed, and soon Holiday was a popular act at such hot spots as the Pod and Jerry's Log Cabin.

> ★★★ **FAST FACT** ★★★
>
> "Strange Fruit" was written by Abel Meeropol, the adoptive father of Julius and Ethel Rosenberg's orphaned sons.

Q. Why were nearly 120,000 American citizens relocated in 1942?

A. Nearly 120,000 Japanese Americans were relocated to isolated camps after Pearl Harbor out of concern that they might assist Japan in a future invasion of the continental United States.

Q. Who founded the Congress of Racial Equality in 1942?

A. James Farmer, Bernice Fisher, James R. Robinson, Joe Guinn, George Houser, and Homer Jack. The Congress of Racial Equality, often called CORE, was formed to fight segregation with peaceful protests. Volunteers gathered outside of theaters, coffee shops, swimming pools, bowling alleys—any segregated public place that African Americans were barred from entering at the time.

I Am Thirsty Too

★ ★ ★ ★ ★ ★ ★ ★ ★ ★ ★ ★ ★

When James Farmer was three or four years old, he was shopping with his mother on a hot day. He was thirsty and saw another (white) child go into a drugstore and come out with a soft drink. Farmer asked his mother if he could get a soft drink too. His mother said no. After they got home that day, she explained to him that black people weren't allowed to go into that store—it was for white people only. Farmer remembered that as the first day he knew he was colored.

TRUE OR FALSE In September 1957, the Little Rock Nine were the first African Americans to attend Little Rock Central High School.

ANSWER True. After the Supreme Court case of *Brown v. Board of Education* struck down the "separate but equal" doctrine in 1955, the NAACP and other civil rights groups had been brainstorming about the best way to push for the desegregation of American schools. Civil rights leaders carefully selected the Little Rock Nine because they believed that these particular students were strong enough to handle the pressures they would face.

⭐ One of the most enduring images of the Little Rock Nine is of Elizabeth Eckford arriving at Central High School on her own and facing angry protestors. All nine were supposed to arrive at the school together, but Elizabeth Eckford had missed the call from the coordinator and arrived by herself.

Q. What was accomplished at the Greensboro sit-ins?

A. Though there had been other sit-ins at other white-only lunch counters, the Greensboro sit-ins began a chain of nonviolent protests against private-sector discrimination. The four African American students from North Carolina Agricultural and Technical State University sat at the Woolworth's lunch counter in Greensboro, North Carolina, on Monday, February 1, 1960. The students were denied service, and the next day 29 students showed up at the counter. Though some stores closed their lunch counters to avoid protests and integration, many stores were serving both whites and blacks by the end of the month.

Q. In 1961, to raise the profile of the civil rights issue, CORE held something they called Freedom Rides. What were they?

A. Bus trips in which multiracial groups stopped and ate at segregated restaurants. A group of African American and white activists took two public buses from Washington, D.C., to the Deep South. At every stop, they sat together in segregated restaurants. In some cities the riders were attacked. By the time they reached Mississippi, most of the participants had been arrested for breaking various segregation laws.

Q. In 1961, which noted civil rights leader became president of the National Urban League?

A. Whitney Young. Young grew up in Kentucky, the son of a high school teacher and a homemaker. During World War II, he worked on a road construction crew as an African American private under the command of white officers. He was promoted within three weeks, which stirred resentment among his peers (both black and white). This experience planted a seed in Young that made him want to work to improve relations between the races. During his tenure as the president of the National Urban League, Young spoke out on major issues, and the League quickly became a major voice in shaping public policy. Young also cultivated strong ties with government and business leaders.

★ Young is credited with coming up with the Urban League's "Street Academy" program, which is an alternative education system designed to prepare high school dropouts for college.

> *"Someone has to work within the system to change it."*
> —Whitney Young, on his role in the civil rights movement

Q. Who was the first African American student to enroll at the University of Mississippi?

A. James Meredith. An Air Force veteran, Meredith made repeated attempts to transfer from all-black Jackson State College to Ole Miss in 1962. The Ole Miss admissions department claimed there were "technical difficulties" with his application. Meredith responded by filing a lawsuit. The case went all the way to the U.S. Supreme Court, which decided in Meredith's favor. Meredith graduated from Ole Miss in 1963.

"We live in a difficult time when it is apparent that men do not love each other."
—Reverend William Arthur Pennington, in his invocation at Meredith's graduation from Ole Miss

TRUE OR FALSE Martin Luther King Jr. was assassinated in Jackson, Mississippi, in June 1963.

ANSWER False. Civil rights leader Medgar Evers was assassinated in Jackson, Mississippi, in 1963. More than 30 years passed before his killer was brought to justice.

★★★ **FAST FACT** ★★★
Martin Luther King Jr. was assassinated in Memphis, Tennessee, in April 1968.

Q. What church was bombed on September 15, 1963?

A. Sixteenth Street Baptist Church in Birmingham, Alabama, was bombed by the Ku Klux Klan. It was the largest African American church in Birmingham. Despite the tragic deaths of four little girls in the incident, more than a decade passed before state authorities charged anyone with the crime. Three Klansmen were tried and convicted, and a fourth suspect died before he could be brought to trial.

★★★ **FAST FACT** ★★★
The four little girls who died that day were Addie May Collins, Denise McNair, Carole Robertson, and Cynthia Wesley.

Q. Who killed three CORE workers in 1964?

A. A mob of Klansmen. Michael Schwerner, Andrew Goodman, and James Chaney were working to get African Americans in Mississippi registered to vote.

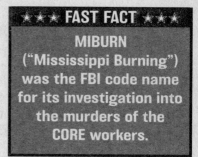

★ ★ ★ **FAST FACT** ★ ★ ★

MIBURN ("Mississippi Burning") was the FBI code name for its investigation into the murders of the CORE workers.

The Klan resented CORE's work and made plans to "take care of" the three. Deputy Sheriff Cecil Price (a Klansman) pulled the three men over on June 17, 1964, and arrested them on a bogus charge. Price released them later that day but secretly followed them after their release. Two more cars full of Klansmen joined the pursuit. The Klansmen shot the CORE workers to death and buried them near an earthen dam.

A jury found 7 Klansmen guilty of violating the civil rights of the murdered CORE workers. The jury acquitted 9 others and was deadlocked on 3 other defendants. None of the Klansmen served more than six years in prison, but the trial was considered a success, as it was the first time anyone had been convicted of a crime against a civil rights worker in Mississippi.

Q. On February 21, 1965, which civil rights activist was assassinated in Harlem?

A. Malcolm X. Malcolm X had once been a devoted Nation of Islam minister, but tensions mounted as his following increased. Malcolm X was assassinated by three of his former fellow Nation of Islam brothers.

Malcolm X

Malcolm X

★ ★ ★ ★ ★ ★ ★ ★ ★ ★ ★ ★

Malcolm X lost his father when he was six years old, and his mother was confined to an institution soon after her husband's death. Imprisoned for burglary at age 21, Malcolm became inspired by the teachings of Elijah Muhammad, leader of the Nation of Islam. Upon his release from prison, he took the last name "X" as a symbol of his stolen African identity and started working as a Nation of Islam minister in Harlem.

After John F. Kennedy was assassinated, Malcolm upset many when he commented that the chickens had "come home to roost" (implying that America lost its leader in a violent fashion because American society is unjust and therefore cursed). Muhammad suspended Malcolm for his controversial comment.

During his suspension Malcolm traveled to Mecca, where he found inspiration in Muslims from all over the globe coming together for worship. Malcolm returned to New York a softened man. He began going by the name El-Hajj Malik El-Shabazz and started the Organization of Afro-American Unity in 1964. Unfortunately, this next mission of his life went unfulfilled: Malcolm was assassinated on February 21, 1965.

Q. How did the tradition of celebrating Kwanzaa begin?

A. Dr. Maulana Karenga, professor and chairman of Black Studies at California State University, Long Beach, came up with the celebration of Kwanzaa as a hopeful reaction to the violence and despair of the riots in the Watts neighborhood of Los Angeles in 1965. Karenga's goal was to strengthen the African American community in California and throughout the country. Kwanzaa is a combination of several different African harvest celebrations. The word *Kwanzaa* derives from an African phrase that means "first fruits." Kwanzaa is a celebration of all that African American culture is and all that it is capable of becoming.

⭐ Kwanzaa does involve gift-giving, but participants are asked to exchange gifts that inspire growth and success. Handmade gifts are encouraged, and accepting a gift means accepting the fulfillment of the promise of the gift. For instance, if a participant receives handmade notecards, by accepting the gift he or she is agreeing to be a careful, beautiful communicator throughout the coming year.

TRUE OR FALSE Jim Crow was a real person.

ANSWER False. Jim Crow was a stock character in minstrel shows. From 1877 to the 1960s, the system of laws to segregate the races in southern states came to be referred to as the Jim Crow system (or Jim Crow laws) after the minstrel character.

Q. Why did 600 African Americans march from Selma, Alabama, to Montgomery, Alabama, on March 7, 1965?

A. To protest the denial of their constitutional right to vote. As the marchers made their way to the capital in Montgomery, law enforcement officers descended upon them near the Edmund Pettus Bridge and attacked them with  batons and tear gas. Footage of the scene was broadcast on ABC television, and an outcry arose across the nation. Two days later, Martin Luther King Jr. led a symbolic march to the Edmund Pettus Bridge. On Sunday, March 21, more than 3,000 protestors left Selma for Montgomery. Additional protestors joined them on the route, and when the group arrived in Montgomery on March 25, it numbered about 25,000 strong.

Kwanzaa's Sacred Principles

* * * * * * * * * * * *

During the celebration of Kwanzaa, each of the seven nights is devoted to one of the following principles:

Unity: This includes unity in the family, community, nation, and race

Self-determination: To define ourselves, name ourselves, create for ourselves, and speak for ourselves

Collective Work and Responsibility: To build and maintain our community together and make our brother's and sister's problems our problems and to solve them together

Cooperative Economics: To build and maintain our own stores, shops, and other businesses and to profit from them together

Purpose: To make our collective vocation the building and developing of our community in order to restore our people to their traditional greatness

Creativity: To do always as much as we can, in the way we can, in order to leave our community more beautiful and beneficial than we inherited it

Faith: To believe with all our heart in our people, our parents, our teachers, our leaders, and the righteousness and victory of our struggles

Q. What was particularly noteworthy about the raid on Greenwich Village's Stonewall Inn in 1969?

A. Two hundred homosexual patrons refused to go quietly. During the 1960s, police in all cities regularly raided places where gays and lesbians gathered. When the Stonewall Inn was raided, however, a 45-minute riot ensued, and the riot repeated on succeeding nights. Gay activists credit the event as the birth of the gay rights movement.

Q. When was the first gay pride parade?

A. June 28, 1970. Parades were held in several major cities—including New York, Chicago, Los Angeles, and San Francisco—to commemorate the one-year anniversary of the Stonewall riots. These 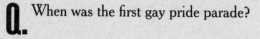 early parades were more like political marches than the bright celebrations that are so common today, but gay pride parades continue to be held on the last weekend in June to celebrate the beginning of the lesbian, gay, bisexual, and transgender (LGBT) movement.

Q. The years 1969 and 1972 were notable for Shirley Chisholm, as well as the United States. Why?

A. In 1969, Shirley Chisholm became the first African American woman elected to Congress. She served in the House of Representatives until 1983. In 1972, she became both the first Democratic woman and the first African American in a major political party to run for president.

Shirley Chisholm

Q. Harvey Milk, the first openly gay politician, was sworn into office for the San Francisco Board of Supervisors on January 9, 1978. How long did he serve?

A. 10 months. On November 27, 1978, Milk and Mayor George Moscone were shot to death by fellow politician Dan White. Milk's assassination would make him a martyr and a symbol of the fight for equality in the LGBT community.

TRUE OR FALSE Massachusetts was the first state to legalize same-sex marriage.

ANSWER True. Massachusetts legalized same-sex marriage in 2004 to comply with the state's Supreme Court ruling in *Goodridge v. Department of Public Health*.

Q. What unique painting was installed in the White House in 2011?

A. Norman Rockwell's *The Problem We All Live With*. The painting depicts U.S. marshals escorting six-year-old Ruby Bridges into a New Orleans elementary school surrounded by angry protesters in 1960. Bridges was the only student in her class that entire school year because angry white parents pulled their children from the school after hearing that it would be integrated.

★ Ruby Bridges campaigned to have *The Problem We All Live With* installed in the White House, and President Obama approved the request. The painting is a popular one, and it often goes out on tour.

SPORTS

★ ★ ★ ★ ★ ★ ★ ★ ★ ★ ★ ★

Whether Americans have lots of leisure time or very little leisure time, they have always found time for sports.

Q. The Chippewa and Sauk gained access to Fort Michilimackinac on June 2, 1763, by distracting British troops with which sport?

A. Lacrosse. The British troops were celebrating King George III's birthday, and the Chippewa and Sauk took notice of this. The Native Americans asked the troops if they would like to watch a game of lacrosse as part of their celebration. The British agreed and were thoroughly enjoying the match when one of the players threw a ball over the fort wall. As the players went inside the fort to retrieve the ball, Native American women passed the weapons they were hiding under blankets on to the players. The Native Americans vastly outnumbered the British, and they quickly killed or captured all of them.

★ The Chippewa and Sauk had resented the British ever since the British victory in the French and Indian War because they refused to trade their muskets and other supplies.

Q. When was the first Kentucky Derby?

A. May 17, 1875. The Kentucky Derby is the oldest continually held sporting event in the United States. In that first exciting race, jockey Oliver Lewis rode Aristides across the finish line before 14 other thoroughbreds.

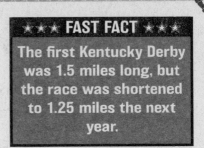

★ ★ ★ **FAST FACT** ★ ★ ★

The first Kentucky Derby was 1.5 miles long, but the race was shortened to 1.25 miles the next year.

Q. Who won the first Rose Bowl game, which was played on January 1, 1902?

A. Michigan defeated Stanford 49–0 to win the first Rose Bowl game, which was played in Pasadena, California.

TRUE OR FALSE The New York Yankees won the first World Series in 1903.

ANSWER False. The American League Boston team defeated the Pittsburgh Pirates to claim the title of World Series champs in 1903.

⭐ The Boston team variously went by "Bostonians" or "Americans" but had no official nickname until 1908, when owner John I. Taylor chose "Red Sox."

Q. What was significant about the 1908 world heavyweight title fight?

A. Flamboyant fighter Jack Johnson won the title in 1908—the first African American to do so.

⭐ Jack Johnson is considered by many to have been the best fighter of all time. When he fought Jim Jeffries on July 14, 1910, he softly batted Jeffries's punches away like nothing, and it seemed as though he could have fought on forever.

Q. What was the first race run at Indianapolis Motor Speedway?

A. You'd be wrong if you thought the first race at the Speedway was a car race. The first race to take place there was a balloon race, on June 5, 1909. The first Indianapolis 500-Mile Race took place on May 30, 1911. Ray Harroun, driving his Marmon Wasp, won that race with an average speed of 74.602 miles per hour. Except for breaks for World War I and World War II, the race has been run every year since.

Q. In which two events did Jim Thorpe win gold medals at the Stockholm Olympics in 1912, only to have them later stripped away after it was discovered that he once received pay for playing baseball (making him a professional athlete)?

A. The pentathlon and decathlon. Thorpe contested the decision of the Olympic committee, pleading ignorance and no intent to deceive anyone. His medals were not restored until 1982, however—nearly 30 years after Thorpe's death.

"Thanks, king."

**—Jim Thorpe, to King Gustav V of Sweden,
after the king told Thorpe he was the greatest athlete in the world**

Q. Members of which major-league baseball team threw the 1919 World Series for money?

1919 Chicago White Sox

A. The Chicago White Sox. Eight members of the Chicago White Sox were kicked out of Major League Baseball for intentionally losing games in the World Series.

⭐ The phrase "Black Sox" is often associated with the scandal that darkened the reputation of Chicago's South Side team, but the term's origins are clouded in mystery. Some hold that it is actually a jab at legendarily cheap team owner Charles Comiskey, who wouldn't cough up the change to launder the team's uniforms.

Q. Who popularized surfing during the 1920s?

A. After winning gold medals for swimming in the 1912 and 1920 Olympics, Hawaiian Duke Kahanamoku performed throughout the world, wowing crowds with his expertise on a 10′ redwood plank.

Q. Which horse won the Lawrence Realization Stakes by 100 lengths on September 4, 1920?

★★★ FAST FACT ★★★

Man o' War died in 1947. His grave is marked with a statue by noted sculptor Herbert Haseltine.

A. Man o' War. The great racehorse beat Hoodwink with a time of 2:40 at Belmont Park. This remains a track record.

Q. When did swimmer Johnny Weissmuller become the first to finish the 100-meter freestyle race in less than a minute?

A. 1922. Best known for his later film roles as Tarzan, Weissmuller swam the 100-

Johnny Weissmuller

meter freestyle race in Alameda, California, in a world-record 58.6 seconds.

Q. When was Jack Dempsey knocked into the press box by an opponent?

A. 1923. Luis Angel Firpo knocked Dempsey over the ropes and into the press box below. The reporters shoved Dempsey back into the ring, and he went on to knock out Firpo in the second round.

⭐ Dempsey being helped back into the ring by reporters was one of the most controversial events in boxing history. Most observers doubt Dempsey would have made it back into the ring on his own in time.

Q. Which female pitcher struck out Babe Ruth and Lou Gehrig in succession on April 1, 1931?

A. Jackie Mitchell. The teen-age Mitchell struck out the

★★★ FAST FACT ★★★

Mitchell learned to pitch from Hall of Famer Dazzy Vance, who was her next-door neighbor.

Babe and the Iron Horse in an exhibition game in Chattanooga, Tennessee. Mitchell's specialty was the curveball, and after that day in 1931, Gehrig and the Babe could both attest to her mastery of it.

Q. Who batted in four runs on September 28, 1930, to bring his season total to 191, an MLB record?

A. Hack Wilson. Playing for the Chicago Cubs, Wilson had a magical season in 1930. His RBI record stands to this very day.

Q. Which American heavy-weight defeated German Max Schmeling at Yankee Stadium in 1938?

A. Joe Louis. When Louis faced Schmeling at Yankee Stadium in a rematch (Schmeling had defeated Louis in 1936), the whole world watched, as the bout was billed as American democracy taking on German fascism. Americans were proud when Louis knocked Schmeling out just two minutes into the bout.

★★★ **FAST FACT** ★★★

During World War II, Louis donated much of his winnings to the armed services.

The Brown Bomber

★ ★ ★ ★ ★ ★ ★ ★ ★ ★ ★ ★

Joe Louis was born Joe Louis Barrow in Alabama in 1914. He was a grandson of slaves and was one-quarter Cherokee. When he was just a child, his family moved to Detroit, Michigan, for its plentiful factory work.

Growing up in Detroit, his friends encouraged him to take up boxing. He started fighting under the name Joe Louis to hide the new activity from his mother. Louis quickly impressed Detroit boxing promoters, who took him under their wings and managed his career.

Joe Louis went on to reign as the heavyweight champ for 12 years—the longest run in organized boxing history.

"Might be a lot wrong with America but nothing Hitler can fix."

—Joe Louis

Q. Which pitcher threw two consecutive no-hitters in 1938?

A. Johnny Vander Meer. Playing for the Cincinnati Reds in his first full season in the majors, Johnny Vander Meer threw his first no-hitter against the Boston Braves on June 11. Four days later, Vander Meer was pitching again, this time against the Brooklyn Dodgers in the first night game at Ebbets Field. In the ninth the crowd was anticipating that Vander Meer might make history, but he kept it interesting. In the bottom of the inning, Vander Meer walked the bases loaded with only one out. Luck was on his side, however, as teammate Lew Riggs threw one player out at home and Leo Durocher flied out to center field to put Vander Meer's second straight no-hitter in the books.

★ Vander Meer's consecutive no-hitters record is among the baseball records least likely to be broken, as in order to do so, a pitcher would have to throw *three* consecutive no-hitters.

Q. When was the first major-league baseball game televised?

A. August 26, 1939. The Dodgers took on the Reds for a double-header at Ebbets Field in Brooklyn, with the Reds taking the first game 5–2 and the Dodgers battling back to win the second 6–1.

★ Owners were at first against the idea of televising games because they were concerned fans would stop coming to the ballparks. The owners were quickly won over by increased exposure and ad revenue, however.

Q. When and where was the color barrier broken in baseball?

A. Baseball's color line was finally shattered as Jackie Robinson made his big-league debut in front of 26,623 fans at Ebbets Field, Brooklyn, on April 15, 1947. Robinson went 0–3 for the Dodgers that day, hitting into a rally-killing double play but also reaching base

later when his speed forced an error. The Dodgers won 5–3. According to Robinson, it wasn't pressure or nerves that kept him hitless—it was the talent of pitcher Johnny Sain.

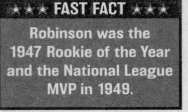

★★★ **FAST FACT** ★★★

Robinson was the 1947 Rookie of the Year and the National League MVP in 1949.

"I don't care if half the league strikes. This is the United States of America and one citizen has as much right to play as another."
—National League President Ford Frick to Cardinals players, who had been planning to strike when the Dodgers came to St. Louis in 1947

TRUE OR FALSE Alice Coachman was the first African American woman to win Olympic gold.

ANSWER True. Coachman, with her high jump at the 1948 Games in London, was the first African American woman to win a gold medal at the Olympic Games.

Q. Who reached base safely on September 27, 1949, to set a major-league baseball record?

A. Ted Williams. Teddy Ballgame reached base safely in 84 straight games in 1949—a streak that remains unbeaten even today.

Q. In what year did the first African American tennis player compete at the U.S. Open?

A. 1950. After fellow player Alice Marble wrote an article in *American Lawn Tennis* magazine advocating that Althea Gibson be allowed to play at the U.S. Open (it was called the U.S. Nationals at the time), Gibson was invited to that year's event. Gibson won her first match but was defeated in the second round.

Althea Gibson

⭐ In 1968, Arthur Ashe became the first African American to win the U.S. Open.

Q. Which NFL quarterback failed to complete a touchdown pass on December 11, 1960— putting an end to his streak of throwing at least one touchdown pass in 47 consecutive games?

A. Johnny Unitas. Unitas's streak began December 9, 1956. His record still stands, and no quarterback has come close to overtaking him.

⭐ The Pittsburgh Steelers drafted Unitas in 1955 but quickly cut him. Signed by Baltimore the following season, Unitas led the Colts for 18 seasons.

TRUE OR FALSE Rocky Marciano retired on April 27, 1956—the first and only heavyweight champ to retire undefeated.

★★★ FAST FACT ★★★

Marciano was the heavyweight champion of the world from 1952 to 1956.

ANSWER True. To this day, with 43 knockouts to his credit, Rocky Marciano remains the only heavyweight champion in boxing history to retire without a defeat or draw.

★★★ FAST FACT ★★★

Robertson averaged 30.8 points, 12.5 rebounds, and 11.4 assists that memorable season.

Q. What was remarkable about Oscar Robertson's 1961–62 season with the Cincinnati Royals?

A. Robertson averaged a triple-double (double-digit points, double-digit rebounds, and double-digit assists) over the entire season—the only player to ever accomplish this feat.

Q. When did the first Daytona 500 take place?

A. February 22, 1959. At first it was believed that Johnny Beauchamp won that first race, but the review of a clip of news-reel three days later revealed that Lee Petty had won by a few feet.

★★★ FAST FACT ★★★

Lee Petty's son Richard Petty went on to become one of the greatest drivers in NASCAR history.

Q. When was the first Super Bowl?

A. The first Super Bowl, called the AFL–NFL World Championship Game, was played in February 1967. The final score was Green Bay Packers 35, Kansas City Chiefs 10.

9 Memorable Super Bowl Halftime Shows

★ ★ ★ ★ ★ ★ ★ ★ ★ ★ ★ ★

1. For Super Bowl XXVI in 1992 at the Hubert H. Humphrey Metrodome in Minneapolis, rival TV station Fox shook things up by running its new comedy show *In Living Color* during halftime. More than 20 million viewers switched from CBS to Fox during the break.

2. At Super Bowl XXX in 1996 at Tempe's Sun Devil Stadium, Diana Ross wowed the crowd by arriving and departing in a helicopter.

3. The halftime show at Super Bowl XXXV in 2001 at Tampa's Raymond James Stadium featured a comedic intro skit by Ben Stiller, Adam Sandler, and Chris Rock, followed by a set list including "Walk This Way" performed by Aerosmith, 'N Sync, Britney Spears, Mary J. Blige, and Nelly.

4. At Super Bowl XXXVII in 2003 at San Diego's Qualcomm Stadium, No Doubt, Sting, and Shania Twain shared the stage. Performances included "Just a Girl" (No Doubt), "Message in a Bottle" (Sting with Gwen Stefani), and "Man! I Feel Like a Woman!" (Shania Twain).

5. At Super Bowl XXXVIII at Houston's Reliant Stadium in 2004, Janet Jackson and Justin Timberlake stunned the country with a "wardrobe malfunction" for the ages.

6. At Super Bowl XXXIX at Jacksonville's ALLTEL Stadium in 2005, Sir Paul McCartney treated the crowd to such hits as "Live and Let Die."

7. At Super Bowl XL in 2006 at Detroit's Ford Field, the Rolling Stones rocked the halftime show on a stage in the shape of the group's recognizable tongue logo. The set list appropriately included the group's classic hit "Start Me Up."

8. At Super Bowl XLI in 2007 at Miami's Dolphin Stadium, Prince revved up the crowd with such hits as "Let's Go Crazy."

9. At Super Bowl XLVI in 2012 at Indianapolis' Lucas Oil Stadium, Madonna wowed the crowd with such hits as "Vogue" and "Like a Prayer."

Q. Who struck out 10 consecutive batters on April 22, 1970?

A. Tom Seaver. In leading the New York Mets to a 2–1 victory over the San Diego Padres on April 22, 1970, Tom Seaver struck out 10 consecutive batters, a league record.

Q. Which hockey player scored an impressive "flying goal" on May 10, 1970?

> **★★★ FAST FACT ★★★**
>
> Orr is the only defenseman in history to ever win the Art Ross Trophy, which goes to the season's leading scorer.

A. Bobby Orr. The goal gave Boston its first Stanley Cup in nearly 30 years. Orr saw the puck go into the net, and he jumped. Ray Lussier's photograph of the moment shows Orr horizontal over the ice with his arms outstretched in victory. It is one of the most iconic images in hockey history.

Q. Which driver won a Formula One race in 1971, making him the only driver to ever win the Daytona 500, the Indy 500, and Formula One?

A. Mario Andretti. Andretti began experimenting with Formula One racing in 1968 and pulled off a win at the South African Grand Prix in 1971.

TRUE OR FALSE The U.S. men's Olympic hockey team defeated the Soviet Union to win the gold medal at the 1980 Winter Games.

ANSWER False. The "Miracle on Ice" occurred at the 1980 Winter Olympics at Lake Placid during a medal-round

American Dreamer

★ ★ ★ ★ ★ ★ ★ ★ ★ ★ ★ ★

Mario Andretti was born in Montona, Italy, in 1940. After World War II, Andretti's hometown fell under Communist rule, and Andretti's family spent seven years living in a displaced persons camp. After finally obtaining U.S. visas, the family moved to Nazareth, Pennsylvania, in 1955.

Upon arriving in the United States, Andretti began working in his uncle's garage. He started racing cars in 1959. Once he won Rookie of the Year honors at the Indy 500 in 1964, there was no stopping Mario Andretti.

men's ice hockey game between the United States and the Soviet Union, but it was not for the gold medal. Coach Herb Brooks and his team defeated the Soviets in one of the greatest sports upsets in history—and went on to win the gold medal against Finland.

Q. In what year did gymnast Mary Lou Retton win a gold medal in the all-around event?

A. 1984. In addition to the gold in the all-around event, Retton won four other medals at the 1984 Olympics in Los Angeles, California. She won more medals than any other athlete competing in the 1984 Olympics.

★ Six weeks before the Olympics, Retton had surgery to repair torn cartilage in her knee. Recovery from the procedure normally takes three months, but Retton sped up the rehabilitation and was ready to compete within three weeks.

Q. Who was the first NFL quarterback to pass for 5,000 yards in a single season?

A. Dan Marino of the Miami Dolphins accomplished this feat in 1984.

★★★ **FAST FACT** ★★★

Two more quarterbacks have now accomplished this feat: Drew Brees of the New Orleans Saints and Tom Brady of the New England Patriots.

Q. Who completed a memorable "Hail Mary" pass in 1984?

A. Doug Flutie of the Boston College Eagles. After the Miami Hurricanes marched down the field to take a 45–41 lead in the closing moments of a game televised nationally the day after Thanksgiving, Flutie consulted his playbook and pulled out a passing "prayer" that would forever be dubbed the Hail Mary. Buried deep in his own territory with only six seconds remaining on the play clock, Flutie avoided a horde of Hurricanes, scrambled to his right, and heaved a pass toward the end zone. The missile sailed 60 yards through a maze of outstretched arms before settling in the grasp of Boston receiver Gerard Phelan, who fell to the field clutching the game-winning pass that delivered a 47–45 victory to the Eagles.

TRUE OR FALSE In 1986, Arnold Palmer won the Masters, his 18th Grand Slam win.

ANSWER False. It was Jack Nicklaus who won the 1986 Masters for his 18th Grand Slam win.

★★★ **FAST FACT** ★★★

Jack Nicklaus still holds the record for most majors with 18.

Q. What skipper raced the *Stars & Stripes* to claim the America's Cup on February 4, 1987?

A. Dennis Conner. Off Fremantle, Western Australia, in 1987, Conner had revenge on his mind, for he had lost the Cup to an Australian team back in 1983. He was determined to win it back, and he did so in thrilling fashion. The *Stars & Stripes* won each of the four Cup races by less than two minutes.

★★★ **FAST FACT** ★★★

The 2013 America's Cup will be held off San Francisco, California. Officials expect the finals to attract hundreds of thousands of spectators.

Q. Whose record did Wayne Gretzky break on October 16, 1989, when he earned his 1,851st career point?

A. Gordie Howe's. When Gretzky retired in 1999, he had 2,857 points, exceeding Gordie Howe's point total by more than a thousand.

"Skate to where the puck is going, not to where it has been."
—Wayne Gretzky's father's sage advice to his son

Q. Which NFL running back rushed for 1,500 yards in 1997—his fourth consecutive year to do so?

A. Barry Sanders. Playing for the Detroit Lions, Sanders rushed for at least 1,500 yards every season from 1994 to 1997.

★★★ **FAST FACT** ★★★

Sanders is the only NFL player ever to rush for 1,500 yards for four consecutive seasons.

TRUE OR FALSE Walter Payton's NFL record for career rushing yards has never been broken.

ANSWER False. Emmitt Smith overtook Payton on October 27, 2002, to lay claim to this record. Smith ended his career with 18,355 yards rushing to Payton's 16,726.

Q. Who was the first African American to medal at a Winter Olympics?

A. Debi Thomas. Thomas won a bronze medal in the figure skating competition at the 1988 Winter Olympics in Calgary.

⭐ Thomas and rival Katarina Witt of Germany both chose Bizet's *Carmen* as the music for their long programs.

TRUE OR FALSE Fenway Park in Boston added lights in 1988.

ANSWER False. It was Wrigley Field that finally turned on the lights against the Phillies on August 8, 1988—the last major-league ballpark to add lights.

> ★★★ **FAST FACT** ★★★
>
> The first game under the lights at Wrigley was called on account of rain after 3½ innings.

Q. Which Dodger hit a home run in his only at-bat of the 1988 World Series?

A. Kirk Gibson. Hampered by a bad left hamstring and a swollen left knee, Gibson was not even in the lineup when the 1988 World Series started. But when his team found itself down 4–3 in the bottom of the ninth with a Dodger on and two outs in

Game One, Gibby was called on to hit against Dennis Eckersley. Gibson looked bad on the first two pitches, but he coaxed the count to 3–2 before reaching out on a backdoor slider and yanking the ball into the right-field seats. A limping Gibby then made his way around the bases as the crowd went wild.

TRUE OR FALSE When Michael Jordan retired for the final time in 2003, he was the highest scorer in NBA history.

ANSWER False. Kareem Abdul-Jabbar holds this record, with 38,387 points to Jordan's 30,652.

Q. Which NCAA basketball team claimed its 11th title in 1995?

A. UCLA. The Bruins won 10 titles from 1964 to 1975 under revered coach John Wooden and added another to their tally in 1995.

Q. Who caught his 23rd touchdown reception on December 29, 2007, to topple the single-season record held for the last three decades by Jerry Rice?

★ ★ ★ **FAST FACT** ★ ★ ★

Jerry Rice played the wide receiver position for a record 20 seasons.

A. Randy Moss. Patriots wide receiver Randy Moss caught a short scoring pass from quarterback Tom Brady to put this record in the books.

SCIENCE AND NATURE

★ ★ ★ ★ ★ ★ ★ ★ ★ ★ ★ ★

From groundbreaking scientific discoveries to medical breakthroughs to a lasting appreciation of nature, science is a leading force in American life.

Q. When were Los Angeles's La Brea Tar Pits discovered?

A. 1769. A group of Spanish explorers were visiting the area and noticed a sticky black substance covering the ground. They christened the area *La Brea*, which is Spanish for *tar*. Later residents of the area used the tar to waterproof their roofs. It wasn't until 1906 that scientists began studying fossils found in the area. Some of these fossils were nearly 50,000 years old, and scientists found preserved fossils stuck in the tar. In 1916, George Allan Hancock, who owned the land, gave it to the city of Los Angeles with the stipulation that it was to be used only for scientific research.

★ Scientists have recovered more than one million fossils from the La Brea Tar Pits—from the littlest insects to short-faced bears that would dwarf modern grizzlies.

Q. What medical breakthrough was announced on October 16, 1846?

A. Thomas Morton, of Boston's Massachusetts General Hospital, first demonstrated the use of ether as a general anesthetic on this date. Before this demonstration, doctors had few options for dulling a patient's pain during surgery.

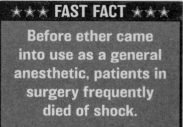

★★★ **FAST FACT** ★★★

Before ether came into use as a general anesthetic, patients in surgery frequently died of shock.

One historian said that surgeons sometimes brought two bottles of whiskey into an operation—one for the patient and one for the surgeon, who had to listen to the patient's screams. Patients were tied down for surgery and felt almost everything.

Q. When was Old Faithful (Yellowstone National Park's most famous geyser) named?

A. Old Faithful was named by members of the Washburn Expedition in 1870. They noted its regular eruptions, and gave it the name it bears today.

Q. What 1889 flood is remembered as the worst flood in United States history?

A. The Johnstown Flood. This historic flood occurred when the dam that had been built to form Lake Conemaugh, for the South Fork Fishing and Hunting Club, broke. The dam was located 14 miles above Johnstown, Pennsylvania, a steel company town tucked into the Conemaugh Valley. Parts of the wall of water that rushed toward Johnstown are estimated to have been nearly 90 feet high. More than 2,000 people died in the tragic flood.

★ Clara Barton and the American Red Cross helped with relief efforts after the Johnstown Flood. It was the first major undertaking of the American Red Cross.

Q. What 1906 earthquake launched modern earthquake science?

A. The 1906 San Francisco earthquake. The 7.9 temblor struck in the early morning hours of April 18 and lasted about a minute. More than 3,000 people were killed, and approximately 225,000 were

> ★★★ **FAST FACT** ★★★
>
> The 1906 San Francisco earthquake is still considered one of the worst natural disasters in U.S. history.

left homeless. Looting was rampant, and police even issued a shoot-to-kill order. California Governor George Pardee called for a thorough investigation of the earthquake, and geology experts came together to form the Lawson Commission. The entire San Andreas fault was mapped as a result of the 1906 San Francisco earthquake.

The Elastic Rebound Theory
★ ★ ★ ★ ★ ★ ★ ★ ★ ★ ★ ★

One member of the Lawson Commission—Henry Fielding Reid of Johns Hopkins University—put forth the elastic rebound theory, which is the underlying principle of modern earthquake science. It holds that plate motion in the earth's crust produces energy just beneath the surface, and this energy elastically distorts the crust. When the crust can't distort any further, it quickly slips along a fault line, then returns to its natural (undistorted) state. This quick slip releases years of pent-up energy and generates seismic waves (the earthquake).

Q. The most powerful volcanic eruption of the 20th century occurred when?

A. June 6, 1912. The eruption of Novarupta, a volcano along the southern coast of Alaska, lasted 60 hours. The sound of the blast reached Juneau (750 miles away) one hour after the eruption began. Ash fell around Novarupta for three days and left drifts that were a foot deep. An ash cloud formed at an altitude of 20 miles and blocked out the sun at midday. The cloud moved across the United States and reached Africa on June 17.

Q. Between 1915 and 1938, Mary Mallon was kept isolated from the general public on North Brother Island off New York City. Why?

A. Mary Mallon was Typhoid Mary. Mary, a carrier of typhoid while immune to the disease herself, worked as a cook and unknowingly spread the disease. When she failed to understand how she could feel perfectly healthy and still be responsible for spreading the disease, it became necessary to quarantine her. She was released in 1909, only to immediately return to working as a cook and infecting people—leading to her re-capture and forced isolation in 1915.

Typhoid bacteria

Q. What virus infected 28 percent of Americans in 1918?

A. Influenza. The flu pandemic of 1918 killed 675,000 Americans. It was the most devastating epidemic in recorded world history. One of the most confounding aspects of the epidemic was that it often killed the young and healthy.

⭐ Some scientists believe the 1918 flu was a bird flu that evolved and jumped to humans. People presumed to have strong immunity had absolutely no immunity because it was a completely new virus.

Q. When was Daylight Saving Time instituted?

A. Many European countries began Daylight Saving Time (DST) after World War I in order to conserve fuel that was needed to produce electric power. On March 19, 1918, the United States enacted DST; it lasted for only seven months, however, because it proved unpopular. During World War II, President Franklin Roosevelt instituted "War Time" (DST), which began on February 9, 1942, and continued until September 30, 1945. After that, it was up to states and localities to choose whether to continue DST.

Q. "The Great Race of Mercy" was a race to acquire antitoxin to stop what outbreak?

A. The 1925 diphtheria outbreak in Nome, Alaska. When diphtheria struck the town's children, it was discovered that no antitoxin was on hand to treat the disease. A shipment could be sent as near as Nenana, but that was still 674 miles away and no direct roads linked the two towns. Thus it was decided that 20 teams of mushers and sled dogs would set out to retrieve the antitoxin. The heroic teams saved the lives of dozens of children.

> ⭐⭐⭐ **FAST FACT** ⭐⭐⭐
>
> **The yearly Iditarod race commemorates the rush to get the diphtheria antitoxin to Nome.**

Q. What natural disaster ravaged the plains between 1931 and 1939?

A. The Dust Bowl. In 1931, a severe drought hit the Midwest and Plains, and dust from the over-grazed, over-farmed land began to blow—causing intense dust storms. The storms would increase in severity and frequency for the next six years, and the drought would continue for seven. Residents of these areas would have to wear makeshift dust masks just to breathe, and their destroyed crops (along with the crashed economy) would send many of them into poverty. It wasn't until 1939 that rain returned—and life improved.

Q. What is April 14, 1935, called in history books?

A. Black Sunday. In the midst of the Dust Bowl, a dust storm (or "black blizzard" as they were called) hit the High Plains. It was severe and massive, and it boasted winds of 40–60 miles per hour. The dust storm blotted out the sun and left residents in pitch-black darkness.

Q. When did the first diet soda hit the market?

A. 1952. No-Cal, the first sugar-free soda, was produced by Kirsch Bottling in Brooklyn, New York. It was intended for people with diabetes. Royal Crown Cola launched Diet Rite in 1958, but the beverage did not get considerable market share until the 1970s, when growing numbers of Americans became concerned about their expanding waistlines.

TRUE OR FALSE Jonas Salk helped wipe out polio in the United States in 1955.

ANSWER True. Dr. Jonas Salk's inactivated polio vaccine (IPV) first appeared in 1955. Today, polio is under control in the developed world, and health authorities are close to controlling the disease in developing countries as well.

Jonas Salk inoculating a patient

Q. In what year did the first commercial nuclear power plant in the United States go online?

A. 1957. Shippingport Atomic Power Station on the Ohio River in Pennsylvania began serving the area's energy needs on December 18, 1957.

TRUE OR FALSE Bill Gates invented the microchip in 1958.

ANSWER False. Jack Kilby invented the microchip while working for Texas Instruments in 1958. With this invention, the foundation for home computers and mobile phones was in place.

Q. Who was the first American in space?

A. Alan Shepard became the first American in space when he piloted the *Freedom 7* capsule on May 5, 1961. Millions watched the televised launch, and Shepard was hailed as a hero after the successful completion of the mission.

> *"The fact that every part of this ship was built by the low bidder."*
> —Alan Shepard, to a reporter who asked what he was thinking as he waited for liftoff

Q. When were the Medicare and Medicaid programs signed into law?

A. July 30, 1965. The Social Security Amendments of 1965 initially provided federal health insurance for poor families and citizens 65 years old and older.

In 1945, President Truman became the first president to honor government-funded health care. To honor Truman's contributions to the cause, President Lyndon B. Johnson enrolled former President Truman as the first Medicare beneficiary as he signed the Medicare bill into law.

Q. What 1969 fire helped ignite the environmental movement?

A. The Cuyahoga River fire. Though river fires were surprisingly common in the United States in the 20th century, this one caught the nation's attention because it occurred just as the environmental movement was gaining momentum. The fire

★★★ **FAST FACT** ★★★

An image of the Cuyahoga fire that ran in *TIME* magazine the month after the 1969 fire was actually an image from a 1952 Cuyahoga River fire.

started as a train was making its way across a railroad bridge over the river in downtown Cleveland. A spark from a broken wheel touched off an explosion in a pool of volatile sludge in the water below. To make matters worse, logs, railroad ties, and other debris tended to collect around the bridge trestles along the slow-moving river. These items provided additional fuel for the flames, and the water itself was full of petroleum and other industrial runoff from steel plants.

Q. When was the National Environmental Policy Act signed, thus creating the Environmental Protection Agency (EPA)?

A. January 1, 1970. In his State of the Union address a couple weeks later, President Nixon expressed his intent to make "the 1970s a historic period when, by conscious choice, [we] transform our land into what we want it to become." Before the end of the year, Nixon created the EPA: a single, independent agency to monitor the environment and respond to environmental threats and issues.

Q. Who organized the first Earth Day in 1970?

A. Senator Gaylord Nelson of Wisconsin. Nelson believed that since we have only one Earth, we need to take care of it. He worked to create Earth Day, the first of which was observed on April 22, 1970. Nelson's grassroots movement led to national legislation such as the Clean Air Act and the Clean Water Act.

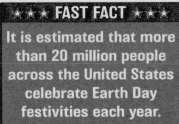

★ ★ ★ **FAST FACT** ★ ★ ★

It is estimated that more than 20 million people across the United States celebrate Earth Day festivities each year.

Q. When was the first American space station launched?

A. May 14, 1973. Designed for long durations, the Skylab station successfully proved that humans could work in space for extended periods. In 1979 Skylab completed its mission. It fell to Earth in thousands of pieces, most of which landed in the Indian Ocean. Some pieces did fall on a sparsely populated part of western Australia.

Q. What noteworthy act did President Nixon sign into law on December 31, 1970?

A. The Clean Air Act. This act required the EPA to draft and enforce regulations to protect citizens from airborne pollutants known to be hazardous to human health.

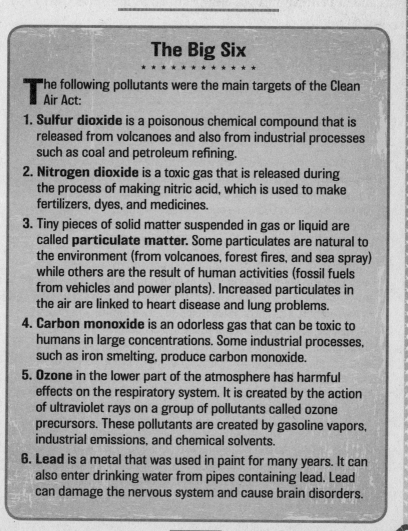

The Big Six

★ ★ ★ ★ ★ ★ ★ ★ ★ ★ ★ ★

The following pollutants were the main targets of the Clean Air Act:

1. **Sulfur dioxide** is a poisonous chemical compound that is released from volcanoes and also from industrial processes such as coal and petroleum refining.

2. **Nitrogen dioxide** is a toxic gas that is released during the process of making nitric acid, which is used to make fertilizers, dyes, and medicines.

3. Tiny pieces of solid matter suspended in gas or liquid are called **particulate matter.** Some particulates are natural to the environment (from volcanoes, forest fires, and sea spray) while others are the result of human activities (fossil fuels from vehicles and power plants). Increased particulates in the air are linked to heart disease and lung problems.

4. **Carbon monoxide** is an odorless gas that can be toxic to humans in large concentrations. Some industrial processes, such as iron smelting, produce carbon monoxide.

5. **Ozone** in the lower part of the atmosphere has harmful effects on the respiratory system. It is created by the action of ultraviolet rays on a group of pollutants called ozone precursors. These pollutants are created by gasoline vapors, industrial emissions, and chemical solvents.

6. **Lead** is a metal that was used in paint for many years. It can also enter drinking water from pipes containing lead. Lead can damage the nervous system and cause brain disorders.

⭐ The EPA estimates that the Clean Air Act has helped the United States decrease total emissions of the six principal air pollutants by more than 41 percent.

TRUE OR FALSE The 1979 nuclear accident at Three Mile Island in Pennsylvania was nearly as bad as the 1986 Chernobyl incident.

ANSWER False. The events at Three Mile Island gripped the country and caused panic throughout the region, but it was

Chernobyl vs. Three Mile Island

★ ★ ★ ★ ★ ★ ★ ★ ★ ★ ★ ★

At Chernobyl, workers were performing a test to see how the reactor would fare in the case of an electrical failure, and a design flaw in the reactor caused a power surge. The surge set off two explosions. As the reactor was not surrounded by any kind of containment structure, the explosions sent a significant amount of radioactive material into the atmosphere.

The incident at Three Mile Island was caused by a failure involving the water pumps. This in turn caused pressure to build up inside the core of the reactor. This pressure caused a relief valve to open. The relief valve failed to close again, and cooling water was released from the reactor. This caused the core of the reactor to overheat. Because the operators did not realize that the plant was experiencing a loss-of-coolant accident, they made conditions worse by further reducing the flow of coolant through the core. Consequently, the nuclear fuel overheated to the point where the long metal tubes that hold the nuclear fuel pellets ruptured and the fuel pellets began to melt.

The Three Mile Island plant was extremely fortunate to have avoided a catastrophic breach of the containment building and the release of massive amounts of radiation into the environment.

no Chernobyl. Though the Nuclear Regulatory Commission (NRC) calls the accident "the most serious in the U.S. commercial nuclear power plant operating history," no lives were lost and the amount of radiation released was within safe lev-
els. On the other hand, at Chernobyl, two workers died the day of the accident and 28 more died of radiation poisoning within weeks. Several thousand others had a greater risk of cancer as a result of the accident.

Q. How many people perished during the 1980 Mount St. Helens eruption?

A. 57. Mount St. Helens, located about 50 miles northeast of Portland, Oregon,

> ★★★ **FAST FACT** ★★★
>
> Some earthquakes leading up to the 1980 Mount St. Helens eruption were close to 5.0 in magnitude.

first began to show signs of an impending eruption in March 1980. For two months, small eruptions and frequent earthquakes warned nearby residents of what was to come. The May 18 eruption produced an avalanche of debris and a cloud of ash and smoke that reached an altitude of more than 12 miles.

Q. What happened in 1982 that made Americans wary of over-the-counter medications?

A. In September 1982, some unknown criminal inserted potassium cyanide into Extra-Strength Tylenol capsules and reshelved the bottles in the Chicago, Illinois, area. Seven headache sufferers were killed. The case was never solved, though in 2011 the FBI collected DNA samples from several suspects, including Unabomber Ted Kaczynski.

Q. When were the first cases of AIDS discovered in the United States?

A. Doctors reported rare types of pneumonia, cancer, and other illnesses among gay men from 1979 to 1981. These illnesses are not usually found in people with healthy immune systems. It wasn't until 1982 that doctors and other public health officials starting using the term AIDS (acquired immune deficiency syndrome) for the opportunistic infections that occurred, namely Kaposi's sarcoma (a type of cancer) and *Pneumocystis jirovecii* (a form of pneumonia). In 1983, scientists named the virus that causes AIDS. The virus was first called HTLV-III/LAV, but the name was later changed to HIV (human immunodeficiency virus).

Q. What led to the 1986 space shuttle *Challenger* disaster?

A. At 73 seconds after the space shuttle *Challenger* lifted off, the shuttle's fuel tanks tore apart, and liquid oxygen and hydrogen spilled out. This created a fireball, and the shuttle tore apart at 46,000 feet. The entire crew perished. The final report blamed the O-ring seals, which were supposed to prevent hot gases from leaking.

★★★ **FAST FACT** ★★★

After the *Challenger* accident, NASA did not launch another space shuttle for two and a half years.

Q. What 1988 occurrence in Yellowstone left Americans concerned about their beloved national park?

A. The Yellowstone fires of 1988. Because many plants in Yellowstone are fire adaptive, fires are allowed to burn and run their course. Despite heavy rains in April and May of

1988, by June the area was in a severe drought. That summer was the driest in the park's recorded history. By July 15, only 8,500 acres had burned in the greater Yellowstone area (out of 2,221,766 total acres), but by July 22, park visitors were beginning to notice the fires; concern was growing. At that point, fire intervention was begun, but high winds and dry conditions fueled the fires. It wasn't until September 11, 1988—when the first snows came—that the fires were dampened and eventually put out.

Though the Yellowstone fires of 1988 were particularly intense, fire plays an integral role in Yellowstone's eco-system. For instance, some of the trees in Yellowstone will not go into their reproductive stages without the intense heat that forest fires produce.

Q. What city was both very hot and very humid in July 1995?

A. Chicago, Illinois. That summer a high pressure air mass originated in the Southwestern desert. As it moved over the Plains states, it picked up moisture because the couple months prior had been particularly wet. When the air mass descended upon Chicago, the humidity was trapped by warmer air above. Thus, Chicago was both hot and humid—a deadly combination—for an entire week. It was more like a Middle

★★★ FAST FACT ★★★

The average temperature in Chicago in July is 84 °F. In July 1995, Chicago endured temperatures as high as 106 °F.

Eastern city than a Midwestern American city. The intense, prolonged heat wave killed more than 700 people.

Q. When was the Human Genome project completed?

A. April 14, 2003. The National Human Genome Research Institution (NHGRI), the Department of Energy (DOE), and their partners in the International Human Genome Sequencing Consortium announced the completion on this date. The U.S. Human Genome Project completed the identification and genetic mapping of the three billion DNA letters in the human genome. Every part of the sequenced genome was made public immediately. It is hoped that through studying the human genome, scientists will discover the functions of all the different genes.

TRUE OR FALSE Hurricane Katrina of 2005 was the deadliest hurricane in United States history.

ANSWER False. The Galveston Hurricane of 1900 (it happened before the hurricane naming system was instituted) was actually deadlier. Approximately 8,000 people died in the  Galveston Hurricane versus the nearly 2,000 who perished during Katrina.

LAW AND ORDER

★ ★ ★ ★ ★ ★ ★ ★ ★ ★ ★

No country can achieve greatness without law and order.

Q. Benedict Arnold, best known for his treason against the United States during the Revolutionary War, was court-martialed on what date?

A. June 1, 1779. The court-martial (though it took place months before his act of treason) is important because most historians agree it embittered Arnold and led him to change sides. Arnold was court-martialed while in command of Philadelphia. While at that post, Arnold had profited from business deals involving troop provisions. Local merchants and politicians believed Arnold's deals were corrupt, and a military board voted to court-martial Arnold. He was cleared of all charges except two but was issued a reprimand by General Washington nonetheless. Soon after the court-martial, Arnold began reaching out to British spies through acquaintances of his wife.

Done In By Pride?

★ ★ ★ ★ ★ ★ ★ ★ ★ ★ ★

Arnold felt unappreciated and misunderstood by his fellow patriots leading up to his court-martial. He believed he had made significant contributions to the patriot cause by co-commanding the expedition that captured Fort Ticonderoga, putting up a valiant effort at Lake Champlain even though he was vastly outnumbered, and, at Saratoga, being shot and then crushed when his horse fell. Each of these efforts was overlooked for various reasons, and Arnold was stung by each perceived slight.

⭐ John André was Benedict Arnold's British cohort as Arnold worked to turn West Point over to the British. Arnold was exposed when André was robbed by AWOL (absent without leave) patriots in the woods north of New York City. The robbers found messages from Arnold hidden in André's boots. André was hanged, while Arnold escaped to Britain.

Q. Three of Thomas Jefferson's accomplishments are etched on his tombstone, by his request. One is the drafting of the Declaration of Independence, and another is the founding of the University of Virginia. What is the third accomplishment?

A. The drafting of the Virginia Act for Establishing Religious Freedom. The Virginia General Assembly passed this

Thomas Jefferson

statute on January 16, 1786. The act stipulated that citizens of Virginia were free to worship as they chose—no person would be compelled to attend any particular church or support any specific church with his taxes.

★★★ **FAST FACT** ★★★

Interestingly enough, Jefferson did not request that his presidency of the United States be etched on his tombstone.

"But it does me no injury for my neighbor to say there are twenty gods or no God. It neither picks my pocket nor breaks my leg."
—Thomas Jefferson

TRUE OR FALSE When John Wilkes Booth killed President Lincoln in 1865, Booth acted alone.

ANSWER False. The Lincoln assassination was part of a broader conspiracy by a group of 10 people, though most of the rest of the conspiracy failed. Vice President Andrew Johnson and Secretary of State William H. Seward were also targeted for assassination, but those assassination attempts were unsuccessful. Seward

John Wilkes Booth

was stabbed but recovered, and Johnson's would-be assassin never got very close to the vice president.

Q. The Volstead Act was passed by Congress on October 28, 1919. What was it also known as?

A. The Prohibition Act of 1919. It gave authorities the power to enforce the 18th Amendment to the Constitution, which banned the manufacture, transportation, and sale of intoxicating beverages. The 18th Amendment took effect in 1920 and heralded an era forever associated with gangsters and speakeasies.

> **★★★ FAST FACT ★★★**
>
> Mississippi, the last dry state, did not repeal Prohibition until 1966.

★ "The Untouchables" were members of a task force led by Elliot Ness. The group was known for being immune to the bribes and corruption prevalent during Prohibition. The supreme test of the group's image came when an agent was offered a bribe by one of Al Capone's men. The agent declined and went straight to Ness.

Prohibition

* * * * * * * * * * * *

The Prohibition movement evolved from the religion-based Temperance movement of the late 19th century, in part as a response to the explosion in the number of saloons around the time of World War I. Many individual counties and states, particularly in the South, had adopted their own local Prohibition laws prior to the national ban on alcohol in 1920. Prohibition quickly became unpopular, and it created a nightmare for law-enforcement officials.

The 21st Amendment repealed the 18th Amendment, making the 21st Amendment the first (and only) amendment to repeal a previous amendment. The 21st Amendment enabled individual states to use their own discretion in deciding when to repeal Prohibition. So, depending on where you lived, Prohibition may not have ended in 1933.

Q. The controversial trial of two Italian American immigrants, Nicola Sacco and Bartolomeo Vanzetti, resulted in their execution on what date?

A. August 23, 1927. Sacco and Vanzetti were alleged anarchists who were accused of murdering two men during an armed robbery in 1920. They were arrested because they were both carrying guns at the time of the murder, though both men had alibis. Many believe their convictions were a result of prejudice against Italian American immigrants and disdain for their extremist beliefs.

★★★ FAST FACT ★★★

Many historians believe that the sophisticated robbery that Sacco and Vanzetti were executed for was actually carried out by professional criminals working for some kind of crime syndicate.

Q. When did the Federal Bureau of Investigation (FBI) open its first crime lab?

A. 1932. The FBI opened its first crime lab in Washington, D.C., with a single employee, agent Charles Appel, who focused on handwriting analysis and analyzing evidence collected from crime scenes.

Q. Whose kidnapping in 1932 led to sensational headlines around the globe?

A. Charles Lindbergh III, son of aviator Charles Lindbergh. Though the Lindberghs fulfilled the demands of the ransom note, the 18-month-old boy was tragically found dead 72 days after the kidnapping. German immigrant Bruno Hauptmann was apprehended after using some of the marked ransom money. He was convicted and later executed.

Charles Lindbergh

Q. Which president tried to pack the Supreme Court in 1937?

A. Franklin Delano Roosevelt. Discouraged by perceived slights by the Supreme Court (the justices invalidated his Agricultural Adjustment Act and struck down the Bituminous Coal Conservation Act, among other setbacks), Roosevelt proposed judicial reforms, including the addition of one justice to the Supreme Court for every one who did not retire by age 70½, with a maximum of five justices added. Roosevelt claimed the reforms were proposed to counteract the courts' overwhelming caseload, but most onlookers perceived it as a grab for power on the part of the president. The infamous "court-packing plan" never went anywhere.

⭐ In 1789, the Supreme Court was established with one chief justice and five associate justices. In 1869, it was decided that three more associate justices were needed to serve the judicial needs of the nation, which had grown significantly in both population and territory since 1789.

Q. When was the only American to be executed for desertion during World War II killed?

Eddie Slovik

A. January 31, 1945. Shortly after arriving in Europe, Eddie Slovik became involved in the fighting around the Hurtgen Forest, where the Allies suffered 33,000 casualties. Eddie was terrified. After submitting numerous requests to be removed from the front lines, he deserted. He turned himself in to authorities the next day and was tried by a court-martial committee, found guilty, and sentenced to death. Many men had been sentenced to death for desertion since the war began, but the United States had not executed one of its own soldiers since the Civil War. Eddie assumed he would stay in jail until the end of the war. Army authorities opted to carry out Slovik's sentence, however. Eddie wrote to General Eisenhower, begging for clemency; Eisenhower refused to rescind the order. On January 31, 1945, Private Eddie Slovik was executed by firing squad.

★ Some historians believe Eisenhower opted not to rescind the order because he received Slovik's letter at the height of the Battle of the Bulge. Historians surmise Eisenhower might have taken offense to Slovik's request for leniency while so many of Slovik's fellow soldiers were dying on the front lines.

Q. When was the first FBI Most Wanted list published?

A. 1950. In late 1949, J. Edgar Hoover of the FBI and William Kinsey Hutchinson of the International News Service (forerunner of United Press International) decided to partner up to catch America's most wanted fugitives. After the first published Most Wanted list received a great deal of attention, the FBI decided to make releasing the list a regular practice.

★★★ **FAST FACT** ★★★

The first criminal apprehended as a result of the publication of the Most Wanted list was Thomas J. Holden, who murdered his wife and her two brothers in addition to being a regular menace to banks and mail trains.

TRUE OR FALSE In 1950, Alger Hiss was convicted of espionage.

ANSWER False. Alger Hiss was actually convicted of perjury, and he served nearly four years in prison. He maintained his innocence throughout his life, but shortly after his death, a collection of documents called the Venona decrypts were declassified. The documents refer to an American working for the Soviets in the U.S. State Department. The documents give the agent the code name Ales and state that Ales traveled with Franklin Delano Roosevelt to the Yalta Conference in 1945 and then flew on to Moscow. Most analysts familiar with the Venona documents believe that Alger Hiss is the only person who fits the description of Ales.

TRUE OR FALSE The 22nd Amendment, which was written into law in March 1951, limits the president to two terms.

ANSWER True. George Washington did not seek a third term (though most historians believe his age was the biggest factor in his decision), and Thomas Jefferson, James Madison, and James Monroe all followed Washington's two-term example. Ulysses S. Grant and Theodore Roosevelt both ran (unsuccessfully) for third terms, and Franklin Delano Roosevelt was famously elected to four terms. The 22nd Amendment was written into law in March 1951 to guard against the United States ever bordering on a monarchy.

Q. Julius and Ethel Rosenberg were the only American citizens to be executed for espionage during the Cold War. When were they executed?

Ethel and Julius Rosenberg

A. June 19, 1953. The Rosenbergs, accused of passing information regarding atomic weapons to the Soviet Union, were convicted of conspiracy to commit espionage during a time of war. They were executed in the electric chair at Sing Sing Correctional Facility. Both maintained their innocence until their deaths. Most historians believe Julius Rosenberg was, indeed, a spy, but his wife was likely innocent. The Rosenbergs left behind two young sons, who were eventually adopted by writer Abel Meeropol and his wife, Anne.

"You are afraid of the shadow of your own bomb."
—Jean-Paul Sartre

Q. What secretive research project resulted in the death of one American in 1953?

A. MKULTRA. This project was developed in response to reports that U.S. prisoners of war in Korea were being subjected to Communist mind-control techniques. From the mid-1950s through at least the early 1970s, mind-altering drugs were given to CIA employees, military personnel, and other government workers, often without the subjects' knowledge or prior consent. More than 30 universities and scientific institutes took part in MKULTRA. At least one American subject—Frank Olson, a U.S. army biological weapons researcher—died in the experiments. Olson was secretly given LSD in 1953. A week later, he fell from a hotel window in New York City following a severe psychotic episode. A CIA doctor assigned to monitor Olson claimed Olson had jumped from the window, but an autopsy performed on Olson's exhumed remains in 1994 found that he had been knocked unconscious before the fall.

Senseless Experiments

★ ★ ★ ★ ★ ★ ★ ★ ★ ★ ★ ★

CIA researchers eventually concluded that the effects of LSD were too unpredictable to be useful, and the agency later admitted that their experiments made little scientific sense. Records on 150 MKULTRA research projects were destroyed in 1973 by order of CIA Director Richard Helms. A year later, *The New York Times* first reported about CIA experiments on U.S. citizens. In 1975, congressional hearings and a report by the Rockefeller Commission revealed details of MKULTRA. In 1976, President Gerald Ford issued an executive order prohibiting experimentation with drugs on human subjects without their informed consent. Ford and CIA Director William Colby also publicly apologized to Frank Olson's family, who received $750,000 by a special act of Congress.

Q. What phrase from President Dwight Eisenhower's January 17, 1961 farewell address gets significant attention to this very day?

EISENHOWER·USA

A. "Military-industrial complex." In his farewell address, Eisenhower warned about allowing the emerging military-industrial complex too much power. In all conflicts before the Cold War, peacetime factories could be transitioned to make war goods relatively easily. Once complex missile systems came into common use, companies and factories that could be devoted only to creating sophisticated missiles were necessary. In the last years of his presidency, Eisenhower saw that this could create a situation where too much of the country's resources were devoted to arms production and defense.

"Every gun that is made, every warship launched, every rocket fired signifies, in the final sense, a theft from those who hunger and are not fed, those who are cold and are not clothed."
—President Dwight D. Eisenhower, in his farewell address

Q. When did District of Columbia residents first vote in a presidential election?

A. November 1964. Before the passage of the 23rd Amendment, D.C. residents were not allowed to vote in presidential elections because the district is not a U.S. state.

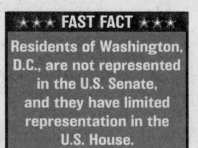

★★★ **FAST FACT** ★★★

Residents of Washington, D.C., are not represented in the U.S. Senate, and they have limited representation in the U.S. House.

Q. What was groundbreaking about the 1966 *Miranda v. Arizona* case?

A. In this landmark case, the U.S. Supreme Court decided that police must thoroughly inform arrested individuals of their rights, including the right to remain silent and the right to a lawyer, and explain that anything said to officials could be used against him or her at trial.

Q. On March 16, 1968, U.S. soldiers murdered 300 civilians. What was this massacre called?

A. The My Lai Massacre. On this date in 1968, the soldiers of Charlie Company stormed the Vietnamese city of My Lai and murdered 300 civilians, including women, children, and the elderly. The incident was exposed by whistleblower Ron Ridenhour. Explanations for the event vary. Some members of Charlie Company claim they were instructed to storm the village and were told there would be no civilians in the area. Others point to the fact that many Charlie Company members had been maimed or killed by landmines in the My Lai area in recent weeks and were pushed to the edge. Still others blame the atrocities on poorly trained draftees and a lack of experienced, professional leaders on the ground in the area. Whatever the reasons behind the incident, My Lai has gone down in history as one of the U.S. military's darkest hours.

> *"Some people—most it seems—will, under some circumstances, do anything someone in authority tells them to."*
> —Ron Ridenhour

TRUE OR FALSE The Pentagon was built in 1969, during the Vietnam War.

ANSWER False. The Pentagon was built in 1943, during World War II. Its purpose was to house the growing War Department. One of the largest office buildings in the world, it is located in Arlington, Virginia, across the Potomac River from Washington, D.C. It was constructed in Virginia because there was no room for it in Washington. Its unique shape is the result of the pattern of the roads surrounding the original site; when a different location was decided upon, the design team went ahead with the chosen plans because of timing concerns. The Pentagon was limited to four stories in height because of a wartime shortage of steel and because it could not obstruct views of the capital city.

Q. When did Nixon identify drug abuse as public enemy No. 1?

A. June 17, 1971. President Nixon announced the creation of the Special Action Office for Drug Abuse Prevention (SAODAP) after naming drug abuse "public enemy No. 1 in the United States." At the beginning of this program, the majority of funding went toward treatment for drug abusers, and not law enforcement.

★★★ **FAST FACT** ★★★

In July 1973, Nixon established the Drug Enforcement Administration.

Q. The federal government attempted to restrain the rights of the press when *The New York Times* began publishing the top-secret Pentagon Papers. When did the Supreme Court rule that the Pentagon Papers could be published?

A. June 30, 1971. For the first time, the federal government had attempted to restrain the press in the name of national security. The Supreme Court ruled that newspapers had the right to publish the Pentagon Papers, which revealed the bungling and deception of U.S. leaders during the Vietnam War.

Q. Who was the first person to be appointed vice president under the 25th Amendment to the Constitution?

Gerald R. Ford

A. Congressman Gerald R. Ford of Michigan. He became vice president in October 1973 after Spiro T. Agnew resigned in disgrace as part of a plea bargain related to charges of income tax evasion and kickback schemes.

★ After Nixon resigned in 1974 and Ford became president, Nelson A. Rockefeller of New York became the second person to be appointed vice president under the 25th Amendment to the Constitution.

Q. Mothers Against Drunk Driving (MADD) was founded in what year?

A. 1980. Candy Lightner founded MADD after her 13-year-old daughter Cari was killed by a drunk driver as she walked home from school. The driver, who was out on bail after being arrested for a hit-and-run three days earlier, had three previous drunk-driving convictions.

TRUE OR FALSE The first execution by lethal injection was carried out in California.

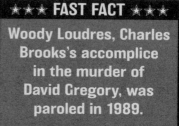

★★★ **FAST FACT** ★★★

Woody Loudres, Charles Brooks's accomplice in the murder of David Gregory, was paroled in 1989.

ANSWER False. The first execution by lethal injection took place in Texas in 1982. Charles Brooks was put to death for the murder of car salesman David Gregory.

Q. On what date did federal agents raid the Mount Carmel Center near Waco, Texas, starting a gunfight that ultimately set up a 51-day siege of the Branch Davidian compound?

A. February 28, 1993. The FBI approached the Branch Davidian compound after reports surfaced about illegal firearms on the premises. As they attempted to serve the warrant and begin their search, shots rang out. The agents maintain that the Branch Davidians fired the first shots, while the Branch Davidians claim that they did not fire until first fired upon. Regardless, a standoff ensued that lasted 51 days. On April 19, 1993, federal agents, in an attempt to force the Davidians out, launched tear gas into the compound. Leader David Koresh and the Davidians began shooting. About six hours after the gassing began, fires erupted inside the compound. (Accusations were made as to which side was responsible for the fires, but later investigations concluded that the fires had been set by the Branch Davidians.) The shooting continued. Firefighters came to the scene but were not allowed to combat the flames for some time out of fear for their safety in the midst of the gunfire. After the smoke cleared, more than 80 people were dead. Koresh was identified by dental records; he had been killed by a gunshot to the head.

The Branch Davidians

★ ★ ★ ★ ★ ★ ★ ★ ★ ★ ★ ★

David Koresh joined the Branch Davidians in 1981. The group had been in existence since 1955, having broken off from the Davidian Seventh-Day Adventists, which itself was a group that split with the Seventh-Day Adventist church more than 20 years before that. Koresh was amiable and flamboyant, easygoing and intelligent. After a face-off with the son of the leader of the Branch Davidians, Koresh ultimately ended up as the group's leader and spiritual guide.

Koresh stockpiled weapons and taught his followers that they should prepare for the end times. He demanded proof of their loyalty and expected them to give their lives for the cause. On February 28, 1993, the end began: Based on reports of illegal arms sales, child abuse, and polygamy, federal agents approached the Branch Davidian compound.

Q. What American building was bombed on April 19, 1995?

A. The Alfred P. Murrah Federal Building in Oklahoma City. Timothy McVeigh had parked a truck in front of the building and detonated a bomb shortly after 9:00 A.M. The explosion killed 168 people and injured more than 500 others. McVeigh was executed on June 11, 2001, and his cohort Terry Nichols is serving a life sentence.

★★★ **FAST FACT** ★★★

The remains of the Murrah Federal Building were eventually razed, and a park now sits on the site.

Q. John Roberts was confirmed as chief justice of the Supreme Court in 2005. How many chief justices preceded him?

A. Sixteen. Since the Constitution stipulates that justices serve for life, there have not been very many chief justices.

5 Infamous Political Scandals

* * * * * * * * * * * *

1. **Teapot Dome:** An oil field reserved for emergency use by the U.S. Navy, Teapot Dome is located on public land in Wyoming. Oil companies and politicians claimed the reserves were not necessary and that the oil companies could supply the Navy in the event of shortages. In 1922, Interior Secretary Albert B. Fall accepted $404,000 in illegal gifts from oil company executives in return for leasing the rights to the oil at Teapot Dome to Mammoth Oil. On April 14, 1922, *The Wall Street Journal* exposed the bribes. In 1927, the Supreme Court ruled that the oil leases had been illegally obtained, and the U.S. Navy regained control of Teapot Dome. Fall was found guilty of bribery in 1929, fined $100,000, and sentenced to one year in prison.

2. **Chappaquiddick:** On July 18, 1969, Senator Edward M. Kennedy attended a party on Chappaquiddick Island in Massachusetts. He left the party with 29-year-old Mary Jo Kopechne. Soon after leaving the party, Kennedy's car veered off a bridge into Poucha Pond. Kennedy said he tried to rescue Kopechne, but the tide was too strong. He swam to shore, went back to the party, and returned with two other men. Their rescue efforts also failed, and Kennedy waited until the next day to report the accident, calling his lawyer and Kopechne's parents first. Kennedy pleaded guilty to leaving the scene of an accident, received a two-month suspended jail sentence, and lost his driver's license for a year.

3. **Watergate:** On May 27, 1972, concerned that President Nixon's bid for reelection was in jeopardy, former CIA agent E. Howard Hunt Jr., former New York assistant district attorney G. Gordon Liddy, former CIA operative James W. McCord Jr., and six other men broke into the Democratic headquarters at the Watergate Hotel in Washington, D.C. They wiretapped phones, photographed some documents, and stole others. When they broke in again on June 17 to fix a bug that wasn't working, a suspicious security guard called

the Washington police, who arrested McCord and four other burglars. On August 29, Nixon announced that the break-in had been investigated and that no one in the White House was involved. Despite his efforts to hide his involvement, Nixon was done in by his own tape recordings, one of which revealed that he had authorized hush money paid to Hunt. To avoid impeachment, Nixon resigned on August 9, 1974. His successor, President Gerald Ford, granted him a blanket pardon on September 8, 1974, eliminating any possibility that Nixon would be indicted and tried.

4. **The Keating Five:** After the banking industry was deregulated in the 1980s, savings and loan banks were allowed to invest deposits in commercial real estate. Many savings banks began making risky investments, and the Federal Home Loan Bank Board (FHLBB) tried to stop them. In 1989, when the Lincoln Savings and Loan Association of Irvine, California, collapsed, its chairman, Charles H. Keating Jr., accused the FHLBB and its former head Edwin J. Gray of conspiring against him. Gray testified that five senators had asked him to back off on the Lincoln investigation. These senators—Alan Cranston of California, Dennis DeConcini of Arizona, John Glenn of Ohio, Donald Riegle of Michigan, and John McCain of Arizona—became known as the Keating Five after it was revealed that they received a total of $1.3 million in campaign contributions from Keating.

5. **The Iran-Contra Affair:** On July 8, 1985, President Ronald Reagan told the American Bar Association that Iran was part of a "confederation of terrorist states." However, this didn't stop members of his administration from secretly planning to sell weapons to Iran to facilitate the release of U.S. hostages held in Lebanon by pro-Iranian terrorist groups. Profits from the arms sales were secretly sent to Nicaragua to aid rebel forces, who were known as the contras, in their attempt to overthrow the Sandinista-controlled government. The incident became known as the Iran-Contra Affair and was the biggest scandal of the Reagan administration.

MONEY AND BUSINESS

★ ★ ★ ★ ★ ★ ★ ★ ★ ★ ★

In the United States as everywhere else, money makes the world go 'round.

Q. In what year was the Bank of the United States founded?

A. 1791. As the young nation's first secretary of the treasury, Alexander Hamilton championed the founding of a national bank, which he modeled after the Bank of England. Hamilton thought a national bank was necessary to provide credit and stimulate the economy.

Q. Trade of what Hawaiian product collapsed in 1830?

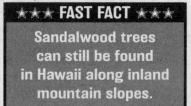

★★★ **FAST FACT** ★★★

Sandalwood trees can still be found in Hawaii along inland mountain slopes.

A. Sandalwood. Chinese markets had a large demand for Hawaiian sandalwood starting in the 1790s. The Chinese used the wood for incense, medicinal purposes, carvings, and architecture. However, by 1830, the trade collapsed because Hawaiian forests were exhausted and the Chinese started obtaining sandalwood from India.

Q. Which labor strike was the first nationwide strike?

A. The Pullman strike of 1894. During the financial panic of 1893, demand for the company's train cars plummeted. Pullman laid off workers and cut the wages of those who remained by 30 percent. To make matters worse, Pullman, who was also his workers' landlord, continued to deduct the same rent from workers'

★★★ **FAST FACT** ★★★

The Pullman strike left 13 strikers dead and 57 others wounded.

paychecks to ensure investors would continue to get the 6 percent return Pullman had promised them. In response, the American Railway Union (ARU), led by Eugene Debs, called for a strike, which began on May 11, 1894. Railroad workers across the nation refused to handle Pullman cars. The strike became a national issue. President Cleveland declared the strike a federal crime and deployed 12,000 troops. The strike ended on August 3, 1894, and many workers and their supporters around the country were devastated as the Pullman employees were forced back to work without having won any concessions.

Q. When did Henry Clay Frick sue Andrew Carnegie in the biggest private lawsuit in the history of the United States at the time?

A. 1900. Carnegie had dismissed Clay as the leader of Carnegie Steel, and Frick lost out on millions as a result. Frick sued Carnegie for the market value of his shares in the company. Frick won the contest, which was billed in the press as the "Battle of the Steel Kings."

> **"Tell Mr. Carnegie I'll meet him in Hell where we are both going."**
> —Henry Clay Frick, in response to Andrew Carnegie's request for a conciliatory meeting

Q. What American company was the world's first billion-dollar corporation?

A. U.S. Steel. J. P. Morgan and Elbert H. Gary incorporated U.S. Steel in 1901 by purchasing Carnegie Steel and combining it with Gary's Federal Steel Company and National Steel Company. U.S. Steel was capitalized at $1.4 billion.

Q. Henry Ford opened Ford Motor Company in 1903. How many other automotive companies opened that year?

A. 88. Nearly 90 other auto manufacturers opened the same year Henry Ford started Ford Motor Company with 12 shareholders and capital totaling $28,000.

Q. What American companies were broken up in 1911 as a result of antitrust proceedings?

A. American Tobacco and Standard Oil. American Tobacco, one of the original 12 members of the Dow Jones Industrial Average, attracted the attention of regulators after it acquired Lucky Strike and more than 200 rival companies. Antitrust proceedings started in 1907, and in 1911, the American Tobacco Company ceased to exist, having been broken up into several different companies. Standard Oil controlled 91% of American oil production in 1904. The U.S. Department of Justice sued

Standard Oil in 1909 under the Sherman Antitrust Act. The Supreme Court ruled against Standard Oil, and the company was broken up in 1911.

The Dow Jones Industrial Average is now pegged to 30 companies, including Coca-Cola, Pfizer, and Walt Disney.

Original Members of the Dow Jones Industrial Average

★ ★ ★ ★ ★ ★ ★ ★ ★ ★ ★ ★

1. **American Cotton Oil:** later became Bestfoods, which is now part of Unilever

2. **American Sugar:** became Domino Sugar in 1900 and is now called Domino Foods, Inc.

3. **American Tobacco:** broken up in 1911

4. **Chicago Gas:** acquired by Peoples Gas, which is now part of Integrys Energy Group

5. **Distilling & Cattle Feeding:** now Millennium Chemicals

6. **General Electric:** the only one of the original 12 still operating under its original name

7. **Laclede Gas:** now operates as the Laclede Group, Inc. but has not been part of the Dow Jones Industrial Average since 1899

8. **National Lead:** now NL Industries but has not been part of the Dow Jones Industrial Average since 1916

9. **North American:** this was an electric utility holding company; it was broken up in 1946

10. **Tennessee Coal, Iron and Railroad:** was acquired by U.S. Steel in 1907

11. **U.S. Leather:** this company was dissolved in 1952

12. **United States Rubber:** became Uniroyal in 1961; merged with B.F. Goodrich in 1986; bought by Michelin in 1990

Q. What was the name of the program Senator Huey Long introduced in 1934?

A. Share Our Wealth. Senator Long of Louisiana wanted the government to redistribute the wealth of the nation's elite. Long's program stipulated that the federal government should give every family an annual income of $2,500, so they could have the necessities of life, including a home and an automobile. The movement fell apart after Long's death.

"I'm a small fish here in Washington.
But I'm the Kingfish to the folks down in Louisiana."
—Huey Long

⭐ Huey Long had aspirations of giving President Franklin Delano Roosevelt a run for his money in the presidential election of 1936, but the colorful senator's life was cut short by an assassin's bullet in Baton Rouge on September 8, 1935.

Q. The wages of California laborers fell in the early 1930s as unemployed migrants streamed into the state. By 1938, they were arriving at a rate of 10,000 a month. What were these workers fleeing?

★★★ **FAST FACT** ★★★

The most dramatic dust storm occurred on May 12, 1934, and carried dust across the East Coast and out to sea.

A. Dust storms. A drought in Colorado, Oklahoma, Kansas, New Mexico, and Texas caused dust storms and created what became known as the Dust Bowl. As the topsoil in these states literally dried up and blew away, unemployed farm workers flooded California. Minimum wage laws were ignored, and contractors took huge cuts of the workers' pay which averaged, in 1935, $289 a year per family.

Q. When did the first McDonald's open?

A. 1955. Ray Kroc, a salesman specializing in milkshake machines, met the McDonald brothers (Richard and Maurice), who ran a California restaurant that served burgers, fries, and milkshakes. The restaurant attracted Kroc's attention because it was the biggest buyer of his milkshake machines: The restaurant was churning out milkshakes 40 at a time. Kroc came up with the idea of franchising the McDonalds' restaurant, and the brothers agreed to the plan. The first restaurant opened in 1955 in Des Plaines, Illinois.

⭐ In 2010, "1955 Burgers" popped up on McDonald's menus in Germany in homage to the first McDonald's burgers. The 1955 Burger sits on a gourmet bun and is topped with lettuce, grilled onions, tomato, bacon, ketchup, and smoky barbecue sauce. The 1955 burger proved to be a huge hit in Germany and all across Europe.

Q. When was the Trans-Alaska pipeline finished and ready for use?

A. 1977. The first oil from the pipeline connecting Prudhoe Bay in the north with the port of Valdez in the south was shipped out on August 1, 1977. Output peaked in 1988 at 2.1 million barrels of oil per day. Current output is less than a million barrels per day.

⭐ The Trans-Alaska pipeline is 800 miles long—the distance from Minneapolis to Oklahoma City. Building it was an impressive engineering feat, as it was constructed in the brutal Arctic wilderness.

ON THE WORLD STAGE

★ ★ ★ ★ ★ ★ ★ ★ ★ ★ ★

**On the world stage since its unique founding,
the United States often leads the charge in world events.**

Q. When was George Washington's farewell address published?

A. September 19, 1796. After years of service to the United States, Washington declined a third term. In his address, Washington stressed the importance of maintaining good faith and justice toward all nations. He advised the new leaders to avoid long-term relations or rivalries with any nation. Washington wanted the government to make decisions for the country on the will of the people—not the will of American allies.

> ★★★ **FAST FACT** ★★★
>
> **Washington thought the United States should take advantage of its isolated location and stay out of foreign affairs.**

Q. What was America's first foreign war?

A. The First Barbary War in 1801. The Barbary pirates had been harassing American ships along the coast of Africa since 1784. Leaders of the African states demanded ransoms for prisoners and tribute money for ships to be left alone. When Thomas Jefferson was serving as a diplomat in London, he asked the ambassador from Tripoli, Abd Al-Rahman, what

> ★★★ **FAST FACT** ★★★
>
> **Acts of piracy occurred again in 1815, leading to the Second Barbary War, whose results mirrored the First Barbary War, only this time in Algiers instead of Tripoli.**

right his country had to demand such payments. The ambassador responded that "it was written in their Koran, that all nations which had not acknowledged the Prophet were sinners, whom it was the right and duty of the faithful to plunder and enslave; and that every mussulman who was slain in this warfare was sure to go to paradise." Attacks on American ships continued. By the time Jefferson assumed the presidency, the United States had warships, and Jefferson sent them "on a cruise" to the African coast. The American ships wreaked havoc in the area until the African states agreed to cease and desist in their acts of piracy.

"It is a settled policy of America, that as peace is better than war, war is better than tribute. The United States, while they wish for war with no nation, will buy peace with none."
—President James Madison, during the Second Barbary War in 1815

TRUE OR FALSE The St. Lawrence Seaway opened in 1912.

ANSWER False. The St. Lawrence Seaway, which was a joint project between the United States and Canada that opened the Great Lakes to ocean-going vessels, opened in 1959.

The United States was resistant to opening the Great Lakes to ocean-going vessels. Faced with the idea that Canada would begin the St. Lawrence Seaway on its own, the United States agreed to take part.

Q. In what year did Standard Oil discover massive amounts of oil in Saudi Arabia?

A. 1938. The company knew there was likely oil in Saudi Arabia, but no one knew where or how much. Standard Oil made a deal with Saudi Arabia in

1933 allowing them the right to explore and drill for oil in return for giving the Saudi government a large sum of money up front and a steady income out of any profits from any oil extracted from Saudi Arabia. Standard Oil's gamble paid off in 1938, when its drillers found impressive amounts of oil at the Dammam Dome near Dhahran.

★ The partnership between Standard Oil and Saudi Arabia was known as the Arabian American Oil Company (Aramco). The Saudis won control of Aramco in 1980, and the company is now called Saudi Aramco.

Q. What 1942 World War II battle in the Pacific is considered to have turned the tide against Japan?

A. Guadalcanal. The United States shifted its focus to Japanese movements on Guadalcanal after it appeared the Japanese were building an airstrip that would give them the capability to disrupt American shipping to Australia. The Americans had more resources at their disposal on Guadalcanal, and they emerged victorious after Japanese forces withdrew from the island. Before Guadalcanal, Japan was on the offensive; after Guadalcanal, they were on the defensive, and the tide never really turned in their favor again.

Q. When was the atomic bomb created?

A. December 2, 1942. Scientists working on the top-secret Manhattan Project completed the world's first self-sustaining nuclear reaction on this date. It took place on a squash court beneath some rusty bleachers at the University of Chicago's long-abandoned Stagg Field. While scores of fellow scientists, officials, and dignitaries looked on, Enrico Fermi's team completed the reaction. Sources say that the mood that day was both exhilarating and terrifying. After the war, Fermi expressed ambivalence about the consequences of his work, which held immense promise for energy production but could also result in complete destruction and utter despair.

Competition to Create Destruction

★ ★ ★ ★ ★ ★ ★ ★ ★ ★ ★ ★ ★

By the close of the 1930s, the Axis powers were said to have begun development of a weapon that would harness atomic energy in order to cause vast, devastating damage. Urged by a letter from physicists Albert Einstein, Leó Szilárd, and others, President Franklin Roosevelt created a committee of scientists to research the feasibility of such a project. This was the first official measure taken by the American government to develop the bomb. Physicists and engineers were recruited from throughout the world to work on what became known as the Manhattan Project.

Q. When was D-Day?

A. June 6, 1944. D-Day was the largest amphibious military operation in history. It involved 6,000 landing craft carrying 176,000 troops, 822 aircraft carrying 18,000 parachutists, and 13,000 aircraft charged with providing air cover and support for the invasion. The successful operation by American, British, and Canadian troops allowed the Allies to liberate northern France within three months. They then advanced into Germany.

Q. When were the atomic bombs dropped on Hiroshima and Nagasaki?

A. On August 6, 1944, the United States dropped an atomic bomb on Hiroshima, Japan, killing as many as 80,000 civilians. More than 30,000 died when the United States dropped a second atomic bomb on Nagasaki, Japan, on August 9, 1944.

Q. What 1960 incident was among the most embarrassing of the Eisenhower administration?

A. The U-2 spy plane incident. The CIA had begun sending U-2 planes on secret missions over the Soviet Union in 1956. The CIA felt confident that the Soviets did not have any equipment sophisticated enough to take down one of the spy planes. On May 1, 1960, one of the spy planes disappeared over the Soviet Union. The CIA assured President Eisenhower that even if the plane had been shot down—the worst-case scenario—the plane would self-destruct in such a way that no one would ever figure out what it was, and the pilot had been trained to kill himself if such a situation ever arose. Eisenhower delivered an address to the American people in which he mentioned that the United States had lost a weather balloon over the Soviet Union. Soviet leader Nikita Khrushchev trotted out American pilot Gary Powers for all to see, as well as the U-2 wreckage, which was clearly the remains of a spy plane. Eisenhower was forced to sheepishly admit that he had lied.

Q. When did the United States sever diplomatic relations with Cuba?

A. 1961. The United States severed relations after Fidel Castro's government nationalized all American businesses in Cuba.